REVIEWS FOR OTHER BOOKS IN THE "HAUNTED FIELD GUIDE" SERIES FROM WHITECHAPEL PRESS

Troy Taylor, President and Founder of the American Ghost Society, has brought a new level of professionalism to the field with the GHOST HUNTERS GUIDEBOOK, which stands as the best and most authoritative book written to date on ghost investigation. Both beginners and experienced investigators alike should make this book their bible. Taylor gives his readers thorough coverage of the subject and the book is the product of Taylor's own first-hand experiences in numerous investigations. Troy is a careful researcher dedicated to promoting professional, responsible research in a field vulnerable to the media's appetite for the sensational. The GHOST HUNTERS GUIDEBOOK gives the straight savvy. The material is grounded, practical and informative. It comes as no surprise that Taylor's book has received international praise!
ROSEMARY ELLEN GUILEY, author of ENCYCLOPEDIA OF GHOSTS & SPIRITS

SO, THERE I WAS by Troy Taylor and Len Adams is not only a chilling look at the strange happenings and weird events that can occur during ghost tours and investigations, it's also one of the funniest books about the paranormal that has ever been written! Troy and Len (along with Luke Naliborski) present a hilarious, and often spooky, collection of stories from haunted places all over the country. You don't want to miss this one!
DAVID GOODWIN, author of GHOSTS OF JEFFERSON BARRACKS

Troy Taylor's GHOST HUNTERS GUIDEBOOK is the best manual that you can find on the how-tos of ghost hunting and I highly recommend it to anyone who wants to get involved in the paranormal field and see what ghost hunting is all about. Troy presents it like it really is and is careful to let the reader know there is nothing glamorous about being a ghost hunter! He presents the methods, the equipment and the photos in a way that no one else has ever done. Don't miss out on this book!
KEITH AGE, Founder of the LOUISVILLE GHOST HUNTERS SOCIETY & Host of SPOOKED

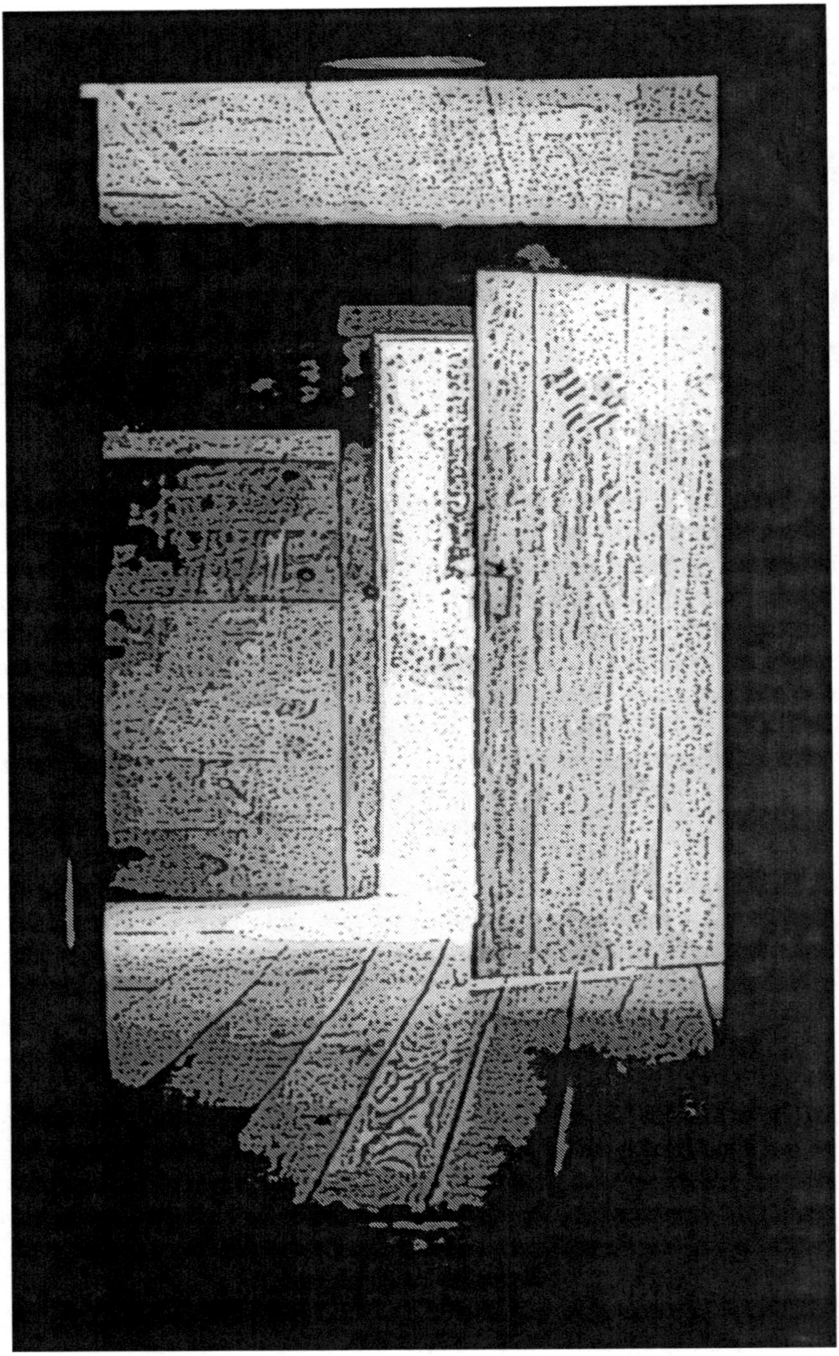

The Haunted Field Guide Series

THE LIGHTER SIDE OF DARKNESS
Misadventures into the Unknown
BY LUKE NALIBORSKI

- A Whitechapel Press Book from Dark Haven Entertainment -

© Copyright 2007 by Luke Naliborski
All Rights Reserved, including the right to copy or reproduce this book, or portions thereof, in any form, without express permission from the author and publisher

Original Cover Artwork Designed by
© Copyright 2007 by Michael Schwab & Troy Taylor
Visit M & S Graphics at http://www.manyhorses.com

Original Photographs by Luke Naliborski
Additional Photograph Credits: Larry Emerick / Others Noted in Text
Front Cover Photograph: John Davis

Editing & Proofreading Services: Jill Hand

This Book is Published By:
Whitechapel Press
A Division of Dark Haven Entertainment, Inc.
15 Forest Knolls Estates - Decatur, Illinois - 62521
(217) 422-1002 / 1-888-GHOSTLY
Visit us on the internet at http://www.prairieghosts.com

First Edition -- September 2007
ISBN: 1-892523-54-X

Printed in the United States of America

THE LIGHTER SIDE OF DARKNESS

By the dismal tarns and pools where dwell the ghouls,
By each spot the most unholy, in each nook most melancholy,
There the traveler meets aghast sheeted memories of the past,
Shrouded forms that start and sigh, as they pass the wanderer by.
White-robed forms of friends long given,
In agony to the Earth and Heaven
- Edgar Allan Poe

The distance that the dead have gone,
Does not at first appear —
Their coming back seems possible,
For many an ardent year.
- Emily Dickinson

Many ghosts, and forms of fright,
Have started from their graves to-night;
They have driven sleep from mine eyes away.
- Henry Wadsworth Longfellow

Dr Ray Stantz: Symmetrical book stacking. Just like the Philadelphia mass turbulence of 1947.
Dr. Peter Venkman: You're right, no human being would stack books like this.
- Ghostbusters (1984)

TABLE OF CONTENTS

ACKNOWLEDGEMENTS -- Page 7
CAST OF CHARACTERS -- Page 8

I. THE BEGINNING -- Page 9

II. GREENWOOD CEMETERY -- Page 21

III. LEMP MANSION --- Page 26

IV. SOUTHERN ILLINOIS FARM HOUSE -- Page 32

V. HAUNTED BUSINESS -- SOUTH COUNTY -- Page 45

VI. ST. LOUIS BED & BREAKFAST -- Page 51

VII. HAUNTING ALTON WITH A LITTLE TLC -- Page 56

VIII. DING, DONG, THE BELL WITCH IS NEVER DEAD -- Page 65

IX. BELLEVILLE, ILLINOIS HISTORIC HOME -- Page 78

X. WAVERLY HILLS SANATORIUM -- Page 84

XI. LINCOLN THEATER -- Page 100

XII. HAUNTED ALTON - A THREE HOUR TOUR -- Page 106

ACKNOWLEDGMENTS

This book would not have been possible without the support of my wife, Heather. I know it's hard to be married to a paranormal investigator because of the long hours and the days away from the family. Heather has been behind me the whole time and has always been there for me when I walked through the front door. She even listens to my constant ghosts stories and actually pretends to be interested! I want to thank my daughter Iris who has not only made me smile in the worst of times, but has also introduced me to the great music of *The Wiggles*. Ok, scratch the last half of that sentence. Even with that fault, she still means the world to me.

I also want to thank my mom Marsha, who always pushed me to succeed. She was always the one who said I could do anything I wanted in life if I put my mind to it. Thanks also to my step-dad Herb, who even though he is in heaven right now, I am sure he's thrilled that I wrote a ghost book. Herb was always fascinated with the idea that there is something else out there.

Thanks to my brothers Sam and Ben for scaring me when I was younger, it helped prepare me for the things I get myself into today.

Thanks to Matt and Len for going into some of the scariest places right by my side. Of course, eventually they'd knock me down and leave me alone in the dark, but they were by my side initially. To kind of quote a certain movie, "You guy's complete me."

And to Kim, Megan and Josh, I thank you for teaming up with me against the legend that is Len Adams. We have to stick together to bring his ego down to earth every once in awhile.

Lastly, thank you Troy Taylor, for involving me in your paranormal world. Whether it was ghostly adventures, tours, conferences or what have you, you always tried to include me. It's an honor to be your friend, colleague and comedic entertainment.

CAST OF CHARACTERS

These are some of the main players you'll hear about. Rather than tell you who each one is every time I mention their name, I figured I'd put their details here.

Luke Naliborski - Hopefully you'll get to know me once you read this book.
Heather Naliborski - My lovely wife and official historian for Prime Investigations.
Len Adams - I've known Len for years and still haven't been able to get rid of him. He is like a wart to me. But it's a good wart. Helped co-found Prime Investigations with me.
Kim Adams - The poor wife of Len as well as a member of Prime Investigations.
Matt Blunt - My best friend of 15 years. Oh, the times we've shared. Handles security for Prime and Alton Hauntings Tours.
Chasidy Holt - Another good friend who I've known for about 15 years. She also introduced me to my wife.
GHOSTS - Investigative team I was a member of with Cathe, Joe, Terry, Miklos, Adam and Jason.
Julie - Member of PRIME Investigations.
"Crazy" Steve - Frequent flyer with our ghostly adventures.
Bill - Photographer, owner of History and Hauntings Book Company and member of PRIME.
Megan and Josh Adams - The children of Len and Kim. They are honorary members of PRIME.

Any other persons mentioned in the book; are mentioned in limited fashion. So unfortunately they didn't make this page. Sorry, maybe next time.

I. THE BEGINNING

A few years back, I heard about this great store in Alton, Illinois, that sells books related to history and hauntings. I knew I had to go there someday, but it was quite a drive from my home, so I didn't know if the day would come or not. That was until my wife and I stayed in Grafton for our anniversary and we made the short drive to Alton. When I walked into the History and Hauntings Book Co., I was immediately captivated. I looked at everything I could get my grimy little fingers on. I immediately selected two books, *The Ghost Hunter's Guidebook* and *Haunted Illinois*. When I took them up to the counter, the gentleman told me about the Alton ghost tours, which I immediately signed up for. I remembered this guy from somewhere, but at the time I couldn't place it. When I laid the books on the counter, the gentleman proceeded to open them up and he started writing on the first page! I was a little ticked off to say the least. What business did this guy have writing in my books? When my wife and I left, I brought it up to her about how rude that was. As we drove away, she looked at what he wrote, and she told me it was his autograph. Using my cunning detective abilities and after examining the photo on the back of the book, I realized that I had just come face to face with Troy Taylor. About a week after I visited the store, I realized where I had seen him before. It was in a classic horror film called *The St. Francisville Experiment*. Not only did I have a brush with an author but also an actor! This turned out to be the start of my frequenting Troy's store. Throughout the years we have built quite a wonderful relationship. We've been on investigations together, and I even had the opportunity to be part of a TLC special he was involved with. But recently, after reading his books, I thought to myself, I could do this too!

I really need to thank everyone who I've met in the paranormal field the past seven or so years. What a great bunch of people to be around! I've met authors, celebrities, investigators, critics, researchers and people who just thirst for paranormal knowledge. It's these people that truly make this field a great team to be a part of. Oh yeah, I've also met Len Adams.

Here's Len and I during a stage show on one of our Dinner Ghost Tours

When I was a kid, if you would have asked me what I wanted to be when I grew up, I would have said, "Troy Taylor!" Just kidding. Actually, it was many years later that I wanted to grow up to be Troy Taylor. The correct answer to the question was that I wanted to be an author. Of course life sometimes doesn't go in the direction that you hoped it would. The only thing I got right is I have a beautiful wife, a gorgeous daughter and some great friends.

I intended on writing a book and eventually began doing it in 2005. I had some stories to tell and really needed to write them down before I forgot everything. (I play hockey, so I get hit in head a little too often.) To show how smart I am, I waited to write it until my daughter was able to walk and get into everything. So obviously my time to write was virtually non-existent. Needless to say, the book had to be put on hold until just recently.

During the 2007 American Ghost Society Conference I had many of my colleagues and friends ask me when my book would be finished. Unfortunately, I didn't have an answer for them. But the fact that these people were interested in what I had to say truly inspired me. Thus, the day has come, and you are reading my first book. I hope you enjoy reading it as much as I enjoyed writing it. Even more than that, I hope you enjoy it as much as I did experiencing it. Oh yeah.....Boo!

Now that you are no doubt on the edge of your seat, let's get the show on the road.

The Beginning

Ever since I was a child, I was always fascinated with the idea of the possibility of ghosts. While most children looked forward to Christmas, I was always more fond of Halloween. It had nothing do with the candy, okay maybe it had a little bit to do with the candy, but the primary reason was to be on edge the entire Halloween season. Halloween also meant scary TV shows and movies would grace my television screen for the festive weeks around Halloween. I have always had a special place in my heart for the *Halloween* movie series. It also meant scary homework assignments at school which helped me feel like doing my homework. More importantly, to satisfy my hunger, I enjoyed hearing the ghost stories people would tell as they attempted to scare each other. I always tried to remember these stories so I could use them myself some day.

I still remember vividly the childhood scare tactics others performed on me. Each new scare pushing my fear and interest to new levels a childhood mind should not have to embrace. For instance, I remember staying at my aunt and uncle's house while my mother worked midnights as a waitress. My uncle, an avid hunter, would come home with various animal carcasses on a nightly basis. One time he came home wearing an animal head and it scared my brothers and me to death. I was about three years old at the time. The first time I saw *The Shining* and *The Exorcist* was also at my aunt and uncle's house. We weren't supposed to be watching them, so although we turned the sound off because we didn't want to get caught, they were still the scariest movies I had ever seen.

I met Linda Blair from *Exorcist* fame during a charity event

While my mother worked midnights, sometimes I'd stay with my other aunt as well. Walking up the creaky exterior steps to get to the dark hallway leading to her apartment was scary enough for a young child. But the story gets better. My aunt had a friend who enjoyed spending time with my brothers and me. Unfortunately, she passed away in the mid-eighties, but her spirit was still there. My aunt's apartment was often visited by a presence that we assumed was the family friend. The usual footsteps would be heard, along with taps on the wall; it was basically a normal type of haunting. I had one experience while staying at the apartment that I will never forget. I was sleeping on the couch in the living room. Right behind the couch was a door that led to the hallway. It was an unused door, so it was locked and the couch was pushed up against it. In mid-sleep I was awakened by a loud rattling and the couch shaking. When I jumped up, I realized the door was rattling so frantically that it was causing the couch to shake. I opened the other door to look out into the hall, and at the very second I peeked out, the door stopped shaking and the hall was empty. There was no way someone could have stopped shaking the door and had time to get out of view before I looked in the hall. Ever since that day, I was uneasy about sitting on the couch, let alone sleeping on it.

I grew up in Belleville, Illinois, in a house that was built in the 1800s. Although I don't remember anything particularly strange happening there, it did have its mysteries. When we started doing some remodeling, we found pages from a German Bible inside a wall along with several old clay marbles. One day, during a bad storm, our gutters got clogged and the water overflowed onto our patio. This patio was made with standard bricks and there was sand and dirt in between the bricks. When the rain hit the bricks, they started to cave inward. The next day when we looked at the damage, we noticed a trapdoor underneath the patio. I regret to say that we never opened this door, so it will remain a mystery. We just covered it back up and continued life as if it were never there. But now that I'm grown up, I constantly think about what could have been under there. Perhaps a treasure, maybe just some emergency canned goods, we'll never know.

Most of my experiences at this house involved hearing different noises at night. This primarily was due to the age of the house and its settling. To a child, though, it was the monsters in my closet trying to get to me. I mastered the long jump by opening the bedroom door, shutting it, turning off the light and getting under the covers in one leap. Sound difficult? Try being a kid who had seen enough scary movies in his short life to know what could be under the bed salivating for his ankles.

When I was in grade school, my brothers and I would walk to and from school every day. It was quite the trek to say the least. Well, there was this one house on our way home, and although I knew nothing about its history, I knew in my heart it was haunted. It was a difficult thing for us to walk past this house everyday. In fact, I don't remember just walking past it too often, it usually seemed to be more of a gallop or full-out sprint to avoid it. Most of the time, even though we walked on the other side of the street so we could be as far away as possible, we would still move as quickly past the house as possible, each time trying not too make any eye contact with the building. Although I never experienced anything remotely paranormal with this house, it did lay the kindling for the fire I was soon to be searching for.

About a half a block away from my house was another home that I was forced to walk past every day as I went to and from school. When I was young, this house was occupied, but as I grew up people would move in and move out at a steady pace. To this day, I can't say for sure that the house was haunted, but I did have some strange experiences.

The first and most startling came in the autumn of 1987. I was 10 years old at the time. Someone had been in the yard of this house cutting down trees and stacking the wood into piles the previous week. We assumed someone had moved into the house and was fixing up the yard. My family had a fireplace and since winter was coming, my stepfather asked my brother and me to go see if we could have or buy some of the wood. It was nighttime when we got the opportunity to go and ask. There had been a light on in the basement for awhile, and it had been turned off by the time we got there. When we knocked on the door, there was no response. So we knocked again. Still no response. As we started to walk away, I heard a shuffling sound from inside, so we stepped back onto the porch. It was at this time that we heard footsteps walking to the door. The strange thing at this point was, the footsteps stopped at the other side of the door, and that was it. The logical next step for whomever or whatever was on the other side of the door would have been to perhaps open it. This didn't happen, so we knocked again. Oddly enough, we heard the footsteps come again, repeating the same movement as before. At this point we got a little scared and high-tailed it home.

    About a week later, we saw a man cutting wood in the yard so we went and spoke with him. We told him how we knocked on the door and heard footsteps but no one ever answered. The man told us he was hired by the city to prune the overgrown trees because no one had lived at that home for quite some time. So what were the sounds we heard? Maybe a little childhood imagination mixed with fear of the house. Maybe an animal found its way in and it thought we were going to let it out. Maybe it was the spirit of a previous tenant who was excited to have some long overdue company. I choose the latter, for the main reason that this experience wasn't the last for me.

    A couple of years later, signs appeared at this house saying it was to be turned into a haunted house for the Halloween season. I found this to be an appropriate use for an already haunted home. Setup for the holiday event went quite well, but not without a few hang-ups. Stories started to float around about the place being a real haunted house. Workers would experience several different phenomena on a daily basis. Lights would be left on. Wood would be moved to different places, doors unlocked, there were unexplainable noises, etc. Perhaps this was a marketing ploy to get people to pay money to go to a fake haunted house expecting it to be a real haunted house. Either way, people would be lined up to see this house for hours every night. I remember joining in on the fun by hiding in the bushes by my house and jumping out at people coming from the Haunted House.

    After the Halloween was over, the workers packed everything up and left. Walking home from school in early November though, I saw something they forgot. If you looked at the front of this house, there were three upstairs windows. On the sill of the middle window was a candle. I remember this candle clear as day because I thought it was strange that the workers would have forgotten something. Now as an adult, I

I met Dan Aykroyd through work one day! The original "Ghostbuster"

guess it really wasn't all that odd, but if I didn't take notice, this story wouldn't have been written. This may sound silly, but I kind of bonded with that candle. I think everyone agrees that as humans, when people tell you something stinks, you smell it, or if you have a bruise that hurts, every once in awhile you have to touch it. This house, although I was scared of it, made me feel compelled to look at it. The candle helped me because when I couldn't fight the urge to look at the house, I was able to focus on that candle. A few days later, I was walking home from school, following my everyday route, and when I looked up to see my old friend the candle in the middle window, it was gone. Seconds later I realized somehow, some way my candle found a new home in the left upstairs window. I didn't ask the candle how it did that, I just ran. Shortly after that instance, the candle appeared in the right upstairs window until one day it was just gone. It did, however, come back one night.

I was outside one evening playing in the front yard. The

house was is in full view so every once in awhile I'd look over at it. I saw my candle again, not just sitting in an upstairs window, this time it had moved to the basement window. There were two peculiar things about my innocent candle now. First, it was moving. Second, the darn thing was lit! It glided along at a downward angle, as if it were moving down a flight of stairs. Although I had been in the house when it was a "Haunted House," I don't remember if there were stairs there or not, but the impression of someone holding it as they descended stairs seemed to be exactly what I saw. Unfortunately, I never saw my candle again, but on occasion, one could look at that basement window and see what appeared to be a flickering light. Years later, the house was torn down and a new one was built there.

    Two stories I was told while growing up, still stick with me today. The first one, told to me by my mother, was a true account of something that happened to her. She was swimming with my aunt one day when it started to storm so badly, they had to rush to my aunt's home. My mother ended up staying the night. She didn't have a change of clothes with her so she had to sleep in her bathing suit. At some point during the night, my mother awoke to see a man standing at the foot of her bed. He wore a white t-shirt and cut-off jean shorts. He just stood there staring until eventually he disappeared. This story really intrigued me, and I loved hearing about it every time I could get my mom to tell it to me. I heard the second tale from a storyteller at a camp I went to in high school. The story spoke of a Native American shape-shifter, whose finger was a sharpened bone with no flesh. She would lure Indian children to her and kill them by using her finger. Of course, before each attack, she would wave the finger in the air in an "S" pattern, and she'd recite a line to the extent of "Su Si Si." Never before have I seen an auditorium full of about 500 teenagers jump in unison. The storyteller and his tale were very entertaining. Hearing these stories, and knowing how interested I was in them, helped me to feel comfortable with sharing my own experiences.
    Often, people who experience unexplained happenings are so concerned with what other people will think of them that they keep their stories inside. I have found that once you start talking about ghosts, one of two things will happen: either the audience

will listen to every word, or they will interrupt you to tell you their own experience. I only hope someday I, too, can have stories to captivate as large a crowd as that storyteller did. Maybe this book will help make that dream come true.

Moving ahead several years to when I was about to graduate from high school brings a few more experiences. Scary movies were abundant now. I could watch them without worrying about my mom catching me. I worked in a video store my senior year, so I made it my business to rent all the horror films I could, regardless of how silly they may have been. It was during this time I saw *Witchboard* and began my fascination with Ouija boards. I know it seems odd that after seeing a movie about people dying as a result of using a Ouija board, I would choose to use one myself, but I was curious. I am very skeptical to this day about them, but I am open to the possibility Ouija boards being a way to communicate with spirits.

My earliest endeavor with these talking boards involved three friends and myself. We were two guys and two girls. When we started talking to a spirit, everyone was on edge wondering what great advice or earth-saving prediction the spirit was going to share with us. Even then, when we find out about this secret, do we share it with the world our keep it to ourselves? One of the girls asked the question of the evening, a question that was going to change my weeks to come. Is the suspense killing you yet? The room was darkened, just a little lamp shedding light from the corner, four individuals' fingers shaking as they touch the viewfinder called a planchette, each finger barely touching it so no one would think they moved it. After taking a deep breath, leaning forward every so slightly so the board would have no trouble hearing her question, it was asked. And I quote, "What will be the initials of my next boyfriend?" It was out there. It had been asked, now we just had to wait. With little hesitation the planchette moved. Across the board it glided until resting upon the "L." It moved a little quicker now, reaching its next destination at the "R." Slowly it glided up and to the right until it found its last resting place on the "N." After thinking about what just transpired before our eyes for a second, it dawned on me. "LRN," that's me! What are the odds that two of the four people using the Ouija board would find love? It was in the stars that night. Naturally we dated, as the spirits predicted, but the flame was short-lived, as were most of my high school romances. However, my interest in this store-bought spirit communicator were only beginning.

My best friend had a Ouija board of his own, so I used it one night with a couple of skeptical friends after work. This experience was a little different than my previous one. We started to communicate with the spirit of a prisoner who died while he was captive. We asked questions for a while and were getting nonsensical answers. To our amazement, the planchette started spinning in a counter-clockwise motion around the whole board. It was moving very fast and we could hardly keep our fingers in place. With the way it was moving, it would have been very difficult for three people to have been able to keep their hands so in sync as to keep the perfect circular motion. I told everyone on the count of three to remove their fingers. As I hit three, we all lifted our fingers and the planchette still finished a half circle without our assistance. The normal thing for an object moving in that manner would have been to just keep on going in a straight line off the table when our fingers were removed. This one, however, continued its circular pattern without our help. That was a pretty strange instance, but the night wasn't over.

While speaking with a different spirit about his life, we heard a noise in the other room. None of us wanted to go check it out alone, so all three of us went. I was in the lead, with Karen behind me and James behind her. We were a fearful train of people slowly walking through the house to where the noise originated. We found nothing and proceeded back to the living room. The train was still intact, only I was no longer the engine; I was now the caboose. Once we got back into the living room, three books stacked next to the Ouija board flew off the table. These weren't magazines or small novels. These books were heavy college textbooks that were completely on the table. They didn't just fall off the edge, they flew about three feet. When we saw this, the train of people started to derail, causing a pileup of scared individuals in the middle of the living room floor. That was it for us using the board that evening. In its place we settled for watching *Witchboard II*.

About a week later, we used the board again and this time we had a light turn off during a conversation with a spirit. These instances are the only experiences of note I have had using a

Ouija board. I am still very interested in this type of phenomena, and I would love to know that this is a true experience of communicating with spirits.

An experiment I have been doing with little success is to use a Ouija board in an allegedly haunted location in complete darkness. I suspend an infrared camera above the board, aiming down at it. I make adjustments so the participants can't see where the pointer is going; only the camera can see what letters are reached. This would cancel out any participant manipulation of the planchette. Feel free to try this yourself. I hope your spirit can spell better and make more sense than those I have encountered while administering this test.

This brief history of my life is what brought me to pursue ghosts. When I was young, I was totally into reading and hearing ghost stories. Now, as an adult, I have my own stories to tell. In this book I have collected the stories of individuals who have experienced unexplained happenings. I am conveying their stories in the way that they were told to me. I will try my best to capture the emotions expressed by each individual. I can't swear that the stories are true, although the people who told them to me insist they are. I will then give an assessment of my experiences, if any, from each location. Rest assured, any experiences I write about involved with these places will be factual. I am also going to share certain rules I learned that each reader should consider when investigating the paranormal. I hope you enjoy this book as I take you into the depths of some extremely haunted, and not-so-haunted, locations.

II. GREENWOOD CEMETERY - DECATUR, ILLINOIS

One of my first semi-investigations would have been when I made my way out to Greenwood Cemetery in Decatur, Illinois for one of Troy Taylor's tours. I can honestly say this was one of my first ventures into a cemetery at night. On our way up to Decatur, my friends Matt Blunt and Adam Winkler and I were like a bunch of giddy kids. We got lost within the first fifteen minutes of our trip. We managed to find our way, though. We even held up our end of the "Man Code" by not asking for directions. Once we got to Decatur we got lost again, but we still managed to find the cemetery with time to spare. With our extra time we decided to stop and eat so we could build up some energy after the long ride. The mood was definitely set for a great evening when the sun started to sink into the horizon. For those of you who do not know the history of this wonderful cemetery, I strongly suggest reading Troy Taylor's book *Where the Dead Walk*.

Upon entering the cemetery gates, there is a large path with mausoleums all around. It reminded me of a miniature Rome. This cemetery was so large that I wish we had more time than we did to be able to look at everything it had to offer. I was very intrigued by the history of the cemetery as well as several of the grave markers. Indians, Civil War soldiers, members of the upper class, members of the lower class, travelers, families, and others have all made Greenwood Cemetery their final resting place. There were two markers I remember vividly. The first was about six or seven feet tall, and looked like a large box. The reason behind this unusually shaped tombstone was the gentleman who rested there was buried inside it standing up. This way, when judgment day came, he would be the first one standing, and would get to heaven quicker. The other distinctive burial spot was a flat mausoleum where the two inhabitants were housed in caskets behind two little double doors. So far it doesn't sound too exciting, but the caskets had glass tops, so upon looking down at them, you'd be staring straight into the inhabitants' faces. This was discovered by a couple of vandals who broke the doors open and pulled one of the caskets out, only to take off running when they got a good look at what it contained.

    I had several sensations while at the cemetery. The first was when we walked down into a valley where a large mausoleum formerly stood. There was an eerie feeling coming over me from both the silence and the coolness of the area. There was no wind and yet I was getting very chilly as cool air moved around me. At that point I didn't know any of the stories about the fact that a mausoleum once stood in the valley we were in. However, I could tell something wasn't right in that area.

    I thought I might have been onto something cult-related when I noticed dead fish laying about on the walkway. However that notion was quickly dispelled when the cause was traced to Mother Nature. There's a river that runs near the path, and due to recent flooding, the fish found their final resting place on the grounds of Greenwood Cemetery. I was let down, but the night wasn't over.

    Toward the end of the evening, people were lingering about on the wide-open walkway by the entrance. This was the entrance where the mausoleums lined the right side. I walked around the mausoleums a little while, taking photos and talking to people. I got a tingling feeling near a tree and decided to take

First Orb photo of my collection

a photo. The photo captured an orb in motion not far from where I was standing. This was the point where I met Terry and showed him my photo. Terry, at the time was a member of GHOSTS (Ghost Hunters of St. Louis Transcendental Society). He looked at the photo and had no explanation for it. When looking at the photo initially, one would think it's the moon or a streetlight. However, if you lighten the photo you will see a large tree trunk behind the orb, canceling out those two theories. Perhaps it's a reflection, but that's not likely since tree bark doesn't reflect light. This was the first anomalous photo I had ever taken.

After showing Terry the photo, Adam, Matt and I walked around a little longer. In fact, we walked away from the entrance a little to take a photo of a mausoleum that had a window broken out. We had noticed before that several people had left and the others were all standing outside the gates, so we figured we had better move along as well. We headed east on the path, and started to turn left at the corner of the row of mausoleums and the wide-open path that led to the gate. When we turned that corner, there was a woman sitting on the steps of a mausoleum. It scared the heck out of me and I know I shouted an explicative. I even made a comment to the woman about how much she scared me. Adam, Matt and I started laughing about the whole thing as we made our way out. As we got to the gate, we started talking about how we noticed the woman on the steps didn't make any kind of response to what had happened. We all turned around and she was gone. In fact, we waited at the gates to see if we weren't the last ones out as we had thought. But everyone was accounted for and the gates were shut behind us. I wish we had paid more attention to details when the incident happened, but we thought everything was normal.

We all talked about the experience on the way home. At first, we were quiet for a while trying to make sense of the thing. I don't remember who broke the ice and started talking about it, but someone did. We all felt that if a person really startles someone, whether they meant to or not, they would probably start laughing or at least they would crack a smile. This lady had a very somber expression on her face. As we got past her and I told her she scared me, she didn't even acknowledge the fact that I spoke to her. And then for her to have had to walk past us to get out, we know she didn't leave the cemetery. Perhaps the reason she stayed is because she can't leave the gates of Greenwood Cemetery.

To this day I still think about this experience. I wonder if maybe she was just someone in the tour even though I didn't recognize her and we did have a rather small group. There were just certain things about her that made me think she wasn't in our group, but rather watching us and wondering why we were there. This may have been my first apparition sighting, but it wouldn't be my last.

Lessons Learned:

1. Pay attention to everything around you. That person we

saw seemed so real to us, yet she quite possibly wasn't.

2. When seeing a ghost, don't curse and wet yourself. It doesn't bode well for your image as a professional.

III. LEMP MANSION - ST. LOUIS, MISSOURI

Shortly after the Greenwood Cemetery experience, I emailed my photo to Terry and he responded with an invite to the Lemp Mansion with the GHOSTS team. I brought my friend Adam along with me, since I didn't know what I was getting into and felt better bringing a friend. It was then that I met Joe and Cathe, founders of the GHOSTS team, Terry, and Miklos, another investigator with the team. This would be the start of my and Adam's involvement with an actual paranormal investigative team.

We started the evening getting to know each other, sharing photos and stories, and just having a good chat while we waited for the Lemp employees to leave. There are several stories about the Lemp Mansion that are very interesting. The most fascinating would be of the suicides that occurred there.

We set up shop in the main bedroom on the second floor and quickly started to place Sony infra-red cameras all over the mansion. Between all the members we had about five video cameras, six EMF detectors, three thermal scanners, six 35mm cameras, and two digital cameras.

The video cameras were set up in different areas where activity had previously been detected. I set my camera up in the dining area on the basement floor. In the past there had been reports of chairs moving, tablecloths being flipped up, silverware clanking, etc. The kitchen is nearby to this dining area and although the staff was gone for the evening, there was still noise coming from there. I had to make note of the common kitchen sounds such as the ice machine as I set my camera up. I didn't want to attribute these noises to anything paranormal upon reviewing my video. After setting up the camera, I proceeded to explore the mansion a little more.

One of the main areas I wanted to see was the attic. I had heard many stories about this part of the building, including the tales of a deformed child who was kept locked up there. Our team, however, was in the midst of setting up surveillance in that area and I couldn't go up there just yet. The Lemp Mansion is a massive structure with many rooms spread over four stories, so the attic wasn't the only place to go. Instead, I walked around taking photos of different rooms and spent quite a bit of time familiarizing myself with the floor plan.

I would have liked to have gone outside to where the horses used to be kept, however this evening we focused our studies indoors. Several stories have been reported about people hearing the sounds of horses walking around the outside of the building. These sounds have been accompanied by horses neighing and men speaking. Investigating the Lemp Mansion's grounds would have to wait until another day.

About two hours had passed, so I decided to go down to the dining area where my camera was recording. The videotape had run out and I replaced it with a new one. I looked around the room a little, just to see if anything seemed out of place. I snapped a few photos and then left the room as to not interfere with any results I may get on tape. Upon returning to the base, I hooked up with Adam and we decided to go up to the attic to take a look around. Keep in mind now, that this was the first investigation for Adam and me, so we were being brave. When we got to the attic, we noticed a video camera was right at the top of the stairs aiming down the hallway. We looked through

View of Lemp Mansion from the street

the viewfinder of the camera and within minutes, we began to see a couple of orbs floating around. We had never seen orbs before; we had just heard about them. I couldn't believe my eyes. I shouted in jubilee. Adam may have wet his pants in excitement. He says he didn't, but I wouldn't admit it either.

After watching the camera for a little while longer, I decided to walk to the end of the hall to try my hand at EVP. For those of you who aren't familiar with EVP, I'll give the short explanation. EVP stands for Electronic Voice Phenomena. Basically, it's a process where voices embed themselves on magnetic tape or digital recording devices. Although you can't hear them when they are initially spoken, upon playback they will reveal themselves. These voices are often clearly audible, but sometimes they are much distorted and one must listen carefully to identify what is being said. In the past, flatbed tape recorders were often used, but as of late, people have begun using digital recorders to pick up EVP. At this investigation, I had a digital recorder that I was using.

I went to the far corners of the attic to conduct my EVP

experiment. I have to admit I was a little scared about being up there by myself. The thing that kept running through my mind was *The Blair Witch Project*. I was half convinced the camera in the hall was going to record some unseen force killing me or something. Nonetheless, my curiosity prevailed and I was able to continue with the investigation. Then I got farther down the hallway to where the motion sensor was located. Well, my movement activated it and sent me jumping. When I got to the end of the hall, I went into the crawl space of the attic and I started asking questions to anyone - or anything - who would listen and hopefully reply. I asked approximately ten questions leaving about five seconds of pause time in between. This five-second block of time was my offer to the spirits to have a chance to speak. Of course, while I am recording the questions, I am unaware of any responses I may have received. I recorded about 10 minutes of questioning and then I left the recorder in the attic and set it to voice activation. This way, it would record only when sound was made. I then made my way back downstairs, all the while remembering the motion sensor that would soon try to frighten me.

The rest of the night was rather uneventful. I took some more photos, got to know the team a little and before too long, Adam and I were ready to call it a night. My first step was to go retrieve my voice recorder. We stopped and looked through the camera viewfinder again, no orbs this time. Adam stayed at the camera while I made my way down the hall. He started hootin' and hollerin' about the orb that was following me and of course my pace picked up a little. I got the recorder and trotted back down the hall. We then made our way to the basement to retrieve my camera. I took a few more photos, said my goodbyes and thanks to the spirits, and my first investigation was officially over.

Paranormal investigators have certain rules that we like to follow. Throughout this book, you will find these rules mentioned periodically. On the way home from this investigation, I introduced myself to a new rule that all should follow. When you are driving from an investigation by yourself, it is not a good time to listen to any EVP recordings you may have.

As I was driving home from the Lemp Mansion, I decided to pull out my digital recorder and review my EVP session. I thought why not save time and listen to it now instead of listening to the radio? There is a point in the session where I ask the following question:

"Is there anything else you'd like to say before I leave?"

As the question completed, I heard a voice abruptly say, "GO!" I nearly swerved off the road. Then I dropped the recorder and swerved into another lane as I was trying to reach down to pick it up off the floor mat.

Over the next few weeks, I reviewed my footage. I didn't get anything noteworthy on the video camera; however after watching a few minutes of it, I think I may have discovered the cure to my insomnia. When I watch the still image, looking closely for any movement whatsoever, it really makes me drowsy. I often found myself nodding off only to hit my head on the desk. I did get an interesting photo on my 35mm camera, though. This is of the dining area downstairs. If you notice on the left side of the screen you will see an orb floating just under the decorative plate. I spent so much time looking at this anomaly, that I didn't pay much attention to the mist coming up off the floor by the chair. I had several other photos from the same angle and this was the only one that had these two anomalies in it.

When I listened to my EVP recordings in greater detail, (and not while driving) I was blown away with what I got. With EVPs, sometimes it's very difficult to decipher what is being said. Often one person will hear one thing and another will hear something totally different. About midway through my questioning I asked:

"Do you know my name?"

Two seconds later, a soft whisper answers with the word "something." I played this for friends and family, not telling them what I heard, to see what they think it says. Most people think it says "Luke," but I feel the fact that they already know the answer to the question greatly influences what they think they hear. A bit after that is where you hear the question I spoke of earlier. This was the question that the spirit answered with "GO." Now keep in mind that when you are doing the questioning, you do not hear the answer. If I had heard a spirit tell me to "go," I probably would have been out the door in a heartbeat. That's one of the neat things about Electronic Voice Phenomena, no matter how much the spirit yells at or threatens you, you continue to ask questions. One has to wonder if this infuriates the spirit. Irritating a spirit may cause it to not want to speak to you anymore or perhaps it will increase activity. I may be on to something with that one. Either way, the experiences I had at the Lemp Mansion paved the way for my advancement in the paranormal field.

Lessons Learned:

1. Teamwork is very important in an investigation. You have to rely heavily on the team for support and free batteries.

2. Do not listen to EVPs while operating a motor vehicle or any other heavy machinery. This was a free public service announcement that comes with your purchase of this book.

IV. OLD FARMHOUSE - SOUTHERN ILLINOIS

My friend Chasidy contacted me about a woman she baby-sits for who was experiencing several haunting activities at her home. In fact, a few times Chasidy and her sister had their own experiences in the house. The stories Chasidy told me were great, and I'll be getting to them later in this chapter, but after talking to the owner, those great stories became incredible stories.

The house was built in the 1800s on an elevated piece of land. The Kaskaskia River runs nearby, and it's surrounded by farmland. This is only speculation of course, but there's a chance the location the house stands on may have been some kind of trading post. The owners found a Spanish Piece of Eight while doing yard work on one occasion, as well as other artifacts. The house itself is a two-story farmhouse. There's a small sidewalk leading up to the side door. Upon entering through the side door, immediately to your right is the staircase leading to the

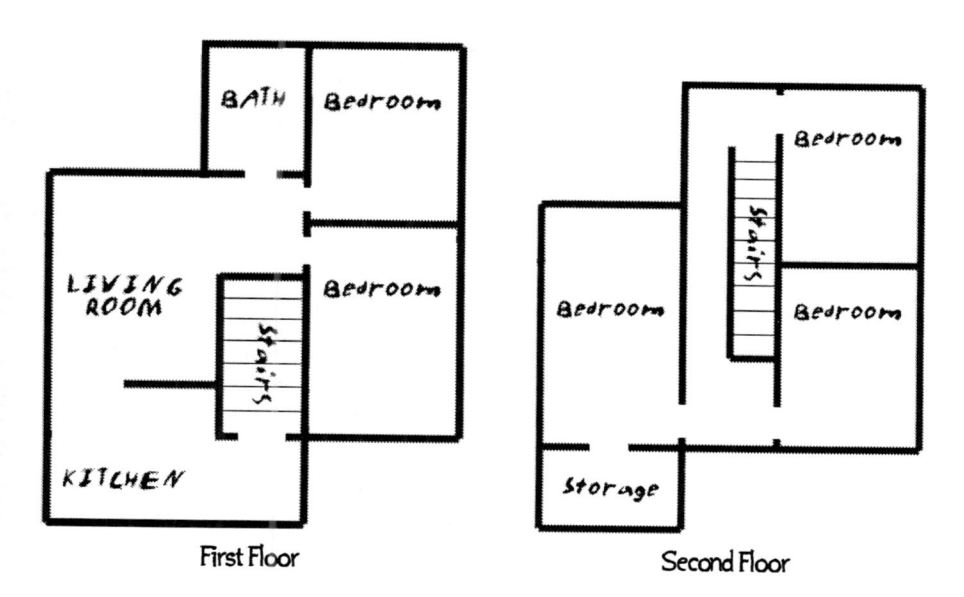

Very disproportionate layout of the home - hand sketched by Luke

second floor. If you walk straight ahead you will enter the kitchen. The living room is off to the right. It's a large room with a very high ceiling. The staircase I previously mentioned runs up behind the north living room wall and over the hallway leading to the bathroom and two bedrooms. Once you reach the top of the stairs, you come to a wall. There's a room to your immediate right. If you turn around and walk parallel to the stairs you'll come to another wall with bedrooms on the left and right. The room on the right also has a small room connected to it. I need to explain the layout of the house so the reader can better understand where things have been happening. I hope my description makes sense.

The activity actually started right away when I first called the homeowner. (We'll call her Sherry for the sake of protecting her identity.) Upon the initial phone interview, our call was abruptly disconnected. Naturally, I called her back. This time, I couldn't get through to her. I waited approximately 15 minutes and called back again. This time, I got through and we started to talk about the experiences she was having, only to be disconnected again! This probably occurred four or five times during the initial interview process. The last time I got through to Sherry, we quickly set up an appointment for me to visit the house and do an in-person interview.

For this initial interview, I brought along my friend Chasidy. She knew the owner as well as the house and of course I didn't want to go alone, so I was excited to have her along with me. I didn't bring a whole lot of equipment. I had a pen and paper which are among my favorite tools. For detecting equipment, I brought a digital camera, a 35mm camera and a Sony Nightshot video camera. When I first got there, I immediately set up my video camera to begin recording while I interviewed Sherry. I asked her what she knows about the house. This is where the story gets very interesting. The following are the stories that she told me.

The History

Sherry lived in the house with her parents and sisters when she was growing up. As most of us did, Sherry would often play with her imaginary friends. She actually had two imaginary friends. There was a little girl that she played with named Sarah. Sarah only stayed outside and would never step indoors. Her other friend was Tommy. Tommy only stayed indoors. Tommy and Sarah were actually brother and sister. These two friends began to take on a role that seemed a little more than imaginary as Sherry began to grow up.

On several occasions as Sherry played with her friends, her parents would come into the room and witness the conversation going on. Although the conversations sounded natural, they almost seemed too real, almost as if her friends weren't just in Sherry's imagination. This feeling may have been proven to be true on one occasion. Sherry was outside playing on a swing. Her mother and sister were in the kitchen preparing the evening meal. From outside, they could hear Sherry carrying on her normal conversation with Sarah. As supper neared completion the mother and sister went to the backdoor to let Sherry know it was time to eat. When they reached the door and peered out, they saw Sherry conversing with the empty swing next to her. (For the record, I am already getting goose bumps just telling this story.) The odd thing was that not only was Sherry talking in the general direction of the swing, but it was also swinging on its own! Sherry's mother called out to her and immediately the swing came to a halt. It wasn't a gradual halt either; it was a sudden stop. Her mother and sister quickly ushered Sherry inside as they began to realize these were not imaginary friends that Sherry had been playing with.

Years went by and Sherry continued to play with little Tommy and Sarah. Eventually, her time in that farmhouse came to an end and her family moved away. Sherry grew older out of state, however she never forgot about her friends back home. After she married and started her own family, she repurchased the old farmhouse. The memories and friends were still there only she didn't know it right away.

Sherry researched the home a little when she moved back to the area. She was able to find out some information about a family that lived there in the early 1900s. When I interviewed her, she told me she found out that a boy and girl died in that house due to a bout with smallpox. What were their names you ask? Would you believe Tommy and Sarah? This really struck home with Sherry. Growing up, this was information she didn't know. What are the odds that a child would have two imaginary friends that shared the same names as two children who died in that very house? I'd have to assume this was no coincidence.

This is the point where the story takes an even stranger twist. As Sherry started to raise her own children in the house, her oldest son began to have conversations with someone in his room. He would have been around three years old at the time. One night, Sherry was able to catch him in the act of talking to someone in one of the upstairs rooms. When she asked what he was doing, he replied that he was talking to his friend Tommy. This almost floored Sherry as she started thinking back to try to remember if she ever told her child about the imaginary friends she had when she was growing up. No matter how hard she thought about it, she couldn't come up with a single instance. She never wanted to tell her children about any of the experiences she had in that house because they were too young and she didn't want to frighten them. Was it possible her son was playing with the same friend? It seems as though the spirits were still there in the house and haven't been able or perhaps haven't wanted to leave.

As the months flew by, her son was still enjoying Tommy's company. However, Sarah wasn't really playing as a big a part as she had in the past. That's not to say she wasn't still there. In fact, she made several appearances every year in a very dramatic fashion. Sherry told me that around five or six times a year a very special look at Sarah would occur. This only happened when someone would pull into the driveway. You had to be watching from the kitchen window. As the visitor would get out of his car and walk across the gravel driveway, they would unknowingly be greeted by Sarah. She would be walking or skipping right alongside the visitor as she escorted him to the door. It's very strange that not only would the visitor not see her, the spectators from inside the house would only see her from the kitchen window. Attempts to view her from other windows were never successful. As stated before though, this didn't occur as frequently as we would wish, so I personally never experienced this amazing sight.

At one time, Sherry rented out the space upstairs. A woman and her young daughter rented the room. Although there weren't any stories of the little girl befriending Tommy or Sarah, she did have her own frightening experience. Sherry was home one weekend along with the young girl. The mother had gone out to run some errands, and Sherry's kids were out with her husband. Sherry was downstairs cleaning up and the girl was upstairs playing in her bedroom. Time went by and the cleaning eventually had Sherry running the vacuum cleaner. This, unfortunately, didn't help the situation as the little girl was screaming at the top of her lungs from her bedroom and the noise of the vacuum covered her cries for help. When Sherry finally heard the shrieks, she dashed up the stairs to find the little girl trapped in one of the crawlspace storage areas. The child had been screaming for a long time, trying to get Sherry's attention. The strange thing is, in order for Sherry to get her out of the crawlspace, she had to unlock the eyehook latch from the outside. This meant whatever trapped the little girl was in the room with her and locked the door behind her. The girl told

Sherry she had gone into the crawlspace looking for a toy, when all of a sudden the door shut behind her and locked. Sherry and the little girl were the only ones home and there was no way the child could have locked the door from the inside. Needless to say, the renters moved out shortly after that.

Other common occurrences were the array of noises the family would hear while going about their daily activities. Sounds of doors closing, knocking noises and the son chatting with Tommy were happening quite frequently. All of these were easy to deal with, but when the sound of footsteps started going up and down the stairs, everyone started feeling more uneasy. It was such a frequent occurrence that eventually the family got used to it. However their comfort level was often pushed to its limits when the footsteps would sound like they were coming towards the listener.

Another incident occurred when Chasidy was babysitting Sherry's kids one afternoon. Everyone was outside in the back yard enjoying the warm weather. As the kids splashed around in the pool, Chasidy looked up to see the curtains in an upstairs window slowly draw back. She saw a little boy gazing through the glass at the children playing in the pool. She watched the boy until he stepped back and the curtains closed. Not a single person was inside the house at that time. Did Chasidy see Tommy wishing he could be outside with the other children? As Sherry told me, Tommy never goes outside. So this story matched a detail of the spirit's behavior.

The stories that Sherry told me really set the tone for the adventures to follow. I actually investigated the home two times after the initial interview and was never let down. It seemed like we were really dealing with a very intelligent haunting. The interaction the spirits have with the family is incredible. It seems they like to let people know they are there in a friendly kind of way. This makes our job as "ghost hunters" a lot easier.

Here's my story from the investigations:

Initial Interview

Right out of the gate, I got an uneasy feeling as I stepped into the house. I always joke that I have no psychic abilities whatsoever. If you take a look around you and find the nearest piece of furniture, that furniture is more psychic than I am. But this uneasy feeling was there and it felt like a heaviness across my chest. It stuck around for about ten minutes as it slowly let go of its hold on me.

The people present were Sherry, her sister, my friend Chasidy and I. Sherry gave us the tour of the home, showing us every room. I took some photos with my digital camera as I normally do during a tour. I also set up my video camera in a side room off one of the upstairs bedrooms. I set the camera in the doorway aiming directly into the room, which was used for storage. I had an odd feeling emanating from behind me as I did some finishing touches on my camera placement. Once the camera was set up and recording, we made our way down to the living room so I could begin asking questions. All four people were present during the interview, sitting on two couches.

As Sherry started telling me the stories as well as answering my questions she was sitting directly to my left. Out of the corner of my right eye, I kept seeing something, but could never catch it to identify it. Finally on about the third or fourth try, I actually caught it by chance. There was a dark shadow that moved across a little hallway about 15 feet from me. It was located directly under the very active staircase. The goose bumps kicked in, but I didn't say anything. I wanted to wait and see if anyone else mentioned it first. No one did. That means that either I was the only one to see it, or everyone else had the same plan as me and wanted to wait for someone else to mention it first.

The rest of the interviewing was pretty uneventful. We heard a couple of sounds, but to me they were just old house sounds. The house settling, the ventilation system, noises from outside, all these seemed to explain the things we heard. It was at this time that I decided to take my friend with me and walk around the house so I could try to explain some things that were happening. I also continued to take photos of the spots I deemed "places of interest."

Eventually we found ourselves wandering upstairs. I was immediately drawn to the area where I set my video camera up prior to questioning Sherry. Chasidy walked to the far side of the room and I stayed by the entrance. The lights were out except for the dim glow of my digital camera. As I snapped a photograph of the room, I glanced down at my camera. It was at this split second that Chasidy took a photo. When her flash lit up the room, I saw a full-figure apparition standing directly in front of me.

One would imagine I saw the spirit of one of the children who passed away in the house, but this was not the case. What I saw him standing in front of me, I became very cold. I spun around and flipped the light switch on only to see there was no one standing in the corner where I had seen the old man. Just then, the window blinds directly outside the bedroom door began to shake. The drawstring for the blinds even began swinging as if something had hurriedly passed by. Chasidy asked what had happened; she could tell by my reaction that I just experienced something strange. I told her I was done upstairs and we should probably head back downstairs for a bit.

I sat back down with Sherry and her sister to ask a few more questions. The questions were mainly about the two children that haunted the home. Sherry's answers were consistent with other stories that she had told me about earlier. I then asked if she knew of any other people who may have died in the house. Sherry had heard that an old man may have passed away there at some point. And where did he pass away you might ask? In the back bedroom where I saw him!

I am a firm believer in power of suggestion. I often feel that giving or getting too much information prior to doing an investigation can lead investigators into a certain direction. It can also lead to generating false conclusions just so an experience can coincide with the knowledge they acquired prior to the investigation. If this were the case here, when I saw the entity in the upstairs bedroom, I would have seen Tommy or Sarah, not an old man. I really feel this experience was a genuine encounter with a full-figure apparition. As you'll read on, it won't be the last time.

The rest of the night was without any more excitement. It was obviously a successful interview due to the amount of information I received as well as the experiences I had. It was only going to be a matter of time before I would come back. Only this time, I was bringing a posse with me.

The Investigation

I scheduled another investigation for a few weeks later. I had most of the GHOSTS team there with me that night. In a strange coincidence, all the lights that lit up the stairwell blew out right before our arrival. Perhaps it was intended to be some mood lighting for us. Or perhaps it was an effort to keep us away from the second floor.

I went over some of the history with the team, but didn't give them much insight to what was going on. After briefing the team, each member started to walk around the house so they could get a feel for what it had to offer. After a quick walkthrough we all met back in the kitchen. Most of the team felt that an area of interest was the upstairs hallway. This was going to be our focal point for the investigation. It was now time to set up our base and equipment.

The kitchen was to be our home base or safe spot, if you will. We had some monitors set up on the kitchen counter with cables running to each video camera we set up around the house. We put cameras at the top of the staircase aiming down the hall towards the window where the blinds moved during the interview. We also had a camera set up inside a bedroom doorway. Its view was across the hallway and into the room where I had seen the old man standing in front of me. Again, I had not mentioned what I saw at this point. This setup was done because it was deemed an active area by the team.

We sat in the kitchen for a while, watching the monitors and seeing orbs move around occasionally. It was at this point that someone had the great idea of having one of our team members sit under the window at the end of the hall. The idea was simple. We would watch both cameras from the kitchen table. If we saw an orb, we would shout out a number. The number one represented an orb to the left of the window. The number two meant an orb was directly in front of the team member. Finally, the number three meant the orb was to the right of the sucker (I mean team member.) The person would then take a photograph, in the direction we yelled, using a 35mm camera. Miklos won the honor of sitting up there in the dark by himself.

The entire time we watched the monitor, we were seeing

orbs move around quite frequently. It was actually quite entertaining as we were yelling numbers out constantly. Of course we had some fun, too, as I was yelling out the number seven and other numbers that meant nothing to the plan we had laid out. The look on Miklos' face as he tried to remember what position I was referring to was priceless.

Miklos had probably spent about 35 minutes leaning against the wall below the window. What really caught my eye was how often he would look over into the room on his left. This was the room where I saw the apparition. Each time, he'd peer over there, get a little shiver and then look back down the hall. We kept asking if he was OK and he would always say that something about that room bothered him. Finally, he had enough; he snapped two quick photos and proceeded to come downstairs. He was quite pale and definitely feeling a bit uneasy.

We then walked outside a bit and took some more photos before calling it a night. This is where the tough part comes. It's time to review the footage. Each member of our team reviews their own footage and we report back to each other with our findings.

The Findings

For those of you who have not done an investigation, reviewing footage can be the dullest thing you could ever imagine! When I have trouble sleeping, all I have to do is throw in one of my investigation tapes and I'm out like a light! If you do this, please try to make sure you are watching it on a soft surface so when your head falls down, you don't hit it on a table or something. You'll thank me later on that one!

Upon reviewing my video footage, I noticed a few orbs at different times. I must say that I am still unsure about orbs. It's tough to tell the difference sometimes from what's paranormal and what's normal. Dust is normal. Bugs are normal. Each of these are often misinterpreted as paranormal. I have seen plenty of orb pictures that are quite possibly spirit forms. Just the same, I have seen tons more that are most definitely dust. If you take a picture and there are so many "orbs" in it that it looks like a ghostly party, it's most likely dust. A pet peeve of mine is when people come up to me with a photo of hundreds of orbs, just so they can get my opinion. I try to be considerate of their feelings (you know how photographers are about taking criticism on their work) when I tell them what I think of their photos. Most of the time they deny each question or point I make. Here are some examples:

I'll say: "It looks really dirty there, sure it's not dust particles?"
They'll say: "Ohhh, no way... It was really clean dirt on the basement floor."

I'll say: "Are you sure it wasn't moisture? It looks like its raining."
They'll say: "No it was a beautiful night. We had the umbrellas to shade us from the moon's harmful rays."

I'll say: "You are investigating by a swamp, could they be bugs?"
They'll say: "No, we had bug repellant on that night. The bugs were dead before they got in view of the cam."

I am now realizing that I have gotten off my subject and onto the much-debated orb identification issue. Let me try to get back to the thought I had a paragraph or so ago.

After reviewing the tape, I did capture a couple "possible" orbs on film. They seemed to have a random flight pattern so it is possible they had intelligence. Most orbs that appear to be dust seem to just kind of float on the breezes of air that may filter through an area. I am not really sure what I may have caught. If only there would have been some other kind of paranormal evidence that would have occurred at the same time as the orb entered the frame. Then I would have something more concrete. The rest of my findings came up empty, unfortunately.

At one point on the video, I have what appears to be an orb. I watched it move along some boxes for a couple of minutes. Then I watched as it stopped on top of a box. It remained there for a bit, until finally the orb stood on its hind feet and began rubbing its paws in front of its little orb face. Then it slowly climbed down the box and ran off into its little orb home. If you

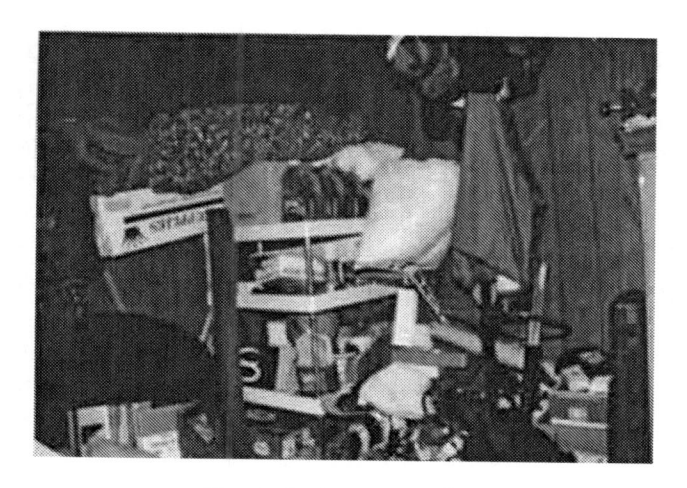

Here is the first picture taken

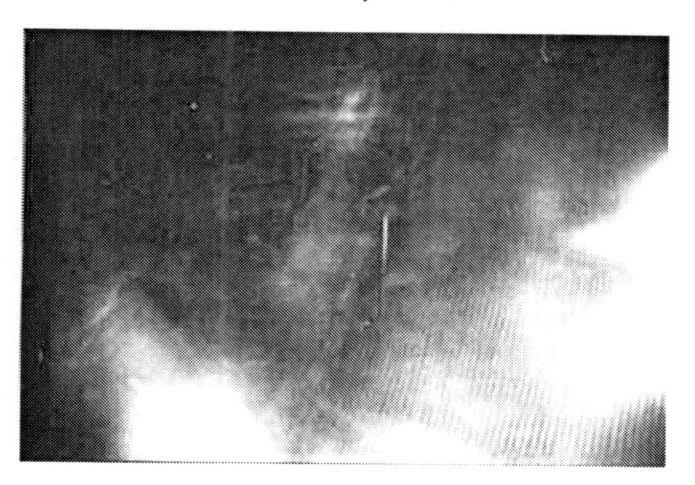

Here is the second photo

haven't figured it out yet, the orb I captured was a mouse. With the infrared light shining on the eyes, it appeared to be a bright glowing orb of light. This could possibly explain some noises they were hearing on the second floor.

Miklos, on the other hand, did have something quite extraordinary happen. When he snapped his two quick photos prior to coming down to the kitchen, he may have captured an entity! The two photos are shown here. Both photos were taken in succession, just a mere five to ten seconds between them. Notice the first one is completely fine. One can make out items as they were stacked about in this room that was being used for storage. Take note of the rectangle box with the crown logo on the left end of it. When you look at the other photo, it appears to have a figure in the center of it. When I initially looked at it, it appeared to have a face, a body and legs. What was even stranger is that it

The Lighter Side of Darkness -- Page 43

seemed to turn towards the camera as the photo was snapped. There is a motion blur where it was looking left and then straight ahead as the shutter snapped. Behind the figure you can see that same box with the crown. This helps the viewer to see that it was taken in the same area and not a totally different place. We did some color modifications and were able to see other faces in the image. However, I am not a believer in photos you have to manipulate in order to see something. I do not consider those photos to be other than an attempt to bring out something that isn't there. However, the figure in the center is definitely there. The image was sent to Kodak for their inspection. As you can tell, the image is rather distorted and we wanted to see what they thought. They sent it back with no explanation as to what it was. If the fine people at Kodak can't explain it, that's good enough for me. Either way, the images are here for you to make your own judgment. (see next page)

No other member had any data that was questionable. Some had possible orbs, but as I said before, without any other data to back them up, we usually dismiss them.

Conclusion

I definitely think this house is haunted. I know what I saw with my own eyes during the initial interview. We have photographic evidence of a possible apparition. We were unable to debunk several of the occurrences in the home. I have since tried unsuccessfully to make contact with Sherry. Hopefully all is well with her and her family.

Lessons learned from this investigation:

1. Try to back up any evidence you find with multiple readings. If you film an orb, look for a temperature drop. If you get a voice on tape, check EMF readings. Obviously, any combination of these will work.

2. Also, even though it may be scary being on the short end of the stick and always being the bait for your team, some of the best things happen to those who persist through their own fear.

V. HAUNTED BUSINESS - SOUTH COUNTY, MISSOURI

Sometimes, through my years of investigations, I have learned that places of business will insist their location is haunted in order to drum up customers. Having a haunted establishment seems to be a very lucrative announcement to make when it comes to being a successful business. Seldom have I come across a business that is haunted, but doesn't want anyone to know about it. Of course there are also some businesses that are completely on the other end of the spectrum. I found - at least I thought I found - a business just like that quite a while ago.

Our team was contacted by the owners of a retail establishment in the South St. Louis area because their store was thought to be haunted. The business was about to open and they wanted us to come out and see if we could explain some strange occurrences. We were very excited about this because we hadn't investigated a business in quite some time.

The owner's son (we'll call him Ricardo) did most of the work to get us out to the location. He was also the one who was going to meet us there. During the initial phone calls, Ricardo told us about the constant activity that was happening all around the store. He spoke of seeing shadows moving across the walls. Workers who were there setting up reported hearing the sound of footsteps walking on the second floor when no one was up there. Doors would open and close by themselves. Things would disappear only to reappear in another location and the sound of voices was a constant. This all seemed like a great opportunity for us to document a lot of activity. We asked what would be a good night to come out and Ricardo said it didn't matter. He assured us that things happened all the time there. So we planned a weekend night when all of our team could make it. With that, everything was set to go.

We always make it our business to arrive about fifteen minutes early to any investigation. This time was no different. The problem was that Ricardo didn't show up until about 45 minutes after he was supposed to open up for us. This adventure was already starting out on the wrong foot. When he pulled into the parking lot, I thought we were going to become ghosts as he nearly ran us over. I am not even sure we got an apology for his lateness, but at least I could tell he was in a hurry to get to us, so it wasn't quite as bad.

Upon entering the front door, Ricardo and his young daughter began giving us a tour of the place. He showed us all the hot spots throughout the building. I was starting to notice a lot of inconsistencies with his stories at this point. There were things that he was telling us in one area which totally went against what he told us in another area. I gave him the benefit of the doubt that it was just a mistake on his part, and I kept it to myself. Sometimes that sort of thing happens to all of us. In the back of my head though, I began to wonder if he was putting on a show for us.

At one point during the tour, he excused himself along with his daughter. He returned about ten minutes later and we began the tour again. We walked into an open room and Ricardo stopped and looked frightened. He slowly raised his hand and pointed towards the other side of the room. "Look!" was all he could muster through fear-ridden lips. We slowly followed his outstretched arm to the other side of the room. Would you believe that the bathroom light was turned on! Seriously! That light was turned on! I have seen a lot of bathrooms in my day, but to have one with a light turned on was definitely something very special to behold.

Now, obviously I am being a little sarcastic with my description of our response. However, I nailed his reaction right on the money. The weird part about the whole thing is I guess he didn't realize that I heard his daughter ask him to take her to the bathroom. I guess he also didn't think that we saw him walk toward the area we were now standing in. Perhaps he didn't think we could put two and two together and realize that quite possibly he turned the light on. Boy did we fool him! I figured it out right away, but again, I didn't point it out at the time. I just made a mental note of what happened and tucked it away for future reference.

Once the tour was over we began going over our game plan for setting up our equipment. I set up my video camera in one of the areas on the second floor that Ricardo said had some activity. I just left my camera recording in that room for the entire night. Other team members placed their cameras in various areas of the second floor. While these cams were recording, the team investigated the first floor hotspots so the upstairs wouldn't be disturbed by us at any point during the investigation.

When I was wandering around on the first floor, I really felt hard-pressed to find any kind of paranormal activity. Normally I can get a bit of a feel for a place within minutes. Not that I am psychic or anything, but I can tell sometimes if a place has activity. These vibes were not happening for me at any point in this building. No matter how hard I tried, it wasn't going to happen at all. The mojo just wasn't flowing that night.

Although I used all sorts of equipment to capture evidence that night, nothing seemed to be working. We didn't have any EMF spikes; no movement was captured on our motion sensor devices. There weren't any temperature drops or visible evidence either. The only thing that was going to salvage this investigation would be our video. Unfortunately we wouldn't know the results until we actually viewed our tapes. I wasn't looking forward to those hours at all.

When the investigation was complete, we all met in the parking lot for a bit. We discussed some of the concerns we had with this business. It definitely seemed like the owners wanted us to say this place was haunted so they could profit from it. Unfortunately, in our book, just because they say its haunted doesn't mean anything to us. At this point in time, the place seemed completely without activity. We decided to go home and review the videos within the next couple of weeks. Upon completion of our reviews, we would get back to each other with our findings. Or we'd get back to each other with our "wastes of time."

During the next week, I began to watch the footage and to say it was boring would be an understatement. There just wasn't anything going on at all. I had two tapes to watch, but after the first one was over, I decided to quit. I put them up on the shelf and forgot about them. That was all about to change a few weeks later.

One night, I was listening to a radio show that was having a live paranormal investigation on the air. I listened to it for a bit and was blown away when I realized they were at the same business we had investigated. Oddly enough, this group was capturing all sorts of activity. The excitement of the disc jockeys was incredible. They were hootin' and hollerin' about all the orbs zooming around. They were hearing tons of unexplainable noises along with all the visuals. My jaw about hit the floor because we were there and we didn't have anything happen. I thought to myself that these guys have got to be kidding, there's no way this place is haunted. Against my better judgment I got the remaining tape from the investigation off the shelf.

I began watching the tape and quickly became bored. So I decided to watch it the 2X speed mode. By doing this, I limited myself to only viewing the tape because there is no sound with this setting. I was willing to take this chance because I was against the idea of even watching the tape in the first place. I didn't even bother having the sound on since I wouldn't be able to hear it.

As I began viewing the footage, it didn't take long for me to start to nod off. I am not sure how long I drifted in and out of consciousness, but I know I was alert at the right time. About 40 minutes into the video, you see the image bounce out of focus. The view that the camera had was just a plain wall. I had a Sony Nightshot camera with the infrared extender. The camera focus was set on the circular glow of infrared light as it was cast upon the wall. During this clip you actually see the camera move down and up, which causes the light to be out of focus for a couple of seconds. The camera actually seems like it moves, but it could be an illusion due to it going out of focus.

When I saw this happen, I immediately rewound the tape and watched it again. Sure enough, it happened and it wasn't just me imagining it happening because I was tired. I then decided to rewind it about ten minutes to watch the tape for a longer period of time. I also decided to turn up the volume this time. I wanted to make sure that nobody walked into the room and perhaps bumped the camera. I let the tape play as I listened to it on my headphones. I wasn't watching the screen at this point because I wanted to focus my attention on the audio instead of the visual.

My heart about stopped when I heard the sound of a woman's voice. I stopped the tape and rewound it again. I still wasn't watching the screen during the playback. I was doing one of those "cock your head at an angle and put your ear near the source" kind of poses. Sure enough, there was that sound again. I rewound it one more time and watched the video along with the audio. I was totally amazed that the woman's voice is at the same exact time as the camera going out of focus.

I listened to that tape several times. I can promise you that there was nobody up on that floor during that timeframe. In fact, you can hear us talking downstairs in some of the video. Not only that, but the voice also sounds "mechanical" and everyone else's voice sounds human. Perhaps "mechanical" isn't the right term, but it does have that type of sound to it. I had to listen to it several more times to try to make out what is said. I came up with two possibilities. I think it either says "I'm alone" or "I'm home." I've had other people listen to it as well and several came up with the same phrases I did.

Now I would like to take a look at the image going out of focus. Was the camera out of focus because it actually was knocked about on the tripod? Or, was the camera out of focus because something or someone was moving around in the room? I personally think that whatever was in that room was trying to let us know it was there however it could. Perhaps the best way for that was to make itself seen and heard. No matter what it was trying to do, it definitely got my attention.

It's crazy to think that I went from declaring that these people were full of you-know-what, to thinking this place may actually be haunted. That clip, although it was the only thing any of our team got, was by far one of the best I've ever captured. I still am not sure about that business being haunted, but I know I can't explain the clip. So even though at first I felt like this was a publicity stunt, now I am not so sure. I then had to file the footage into my "open" case file. Perhaps someday I'll get to go back.

Lessons Learned

1. Never assume anything. When conducting an investigation, do not make a decision until all available evidence has been analyzed. The slightest detail can be missed if you do not have an open mind about the possibilities of a haunting.

2. Do not watch investigation tapes without the audio. Also, try to watch the tapes after you are well rested. If you fall asleep for too long, you could have missed some major development in the paranormal field. Trust me, once you fall asleep, you will NEVER rewind the tape and start over.

VI. HAUNTED BED AND BREAKFAST - ST. LOUIS

    I am going to be very vague with the history on this particular investigation. I'd like to protect the identity of the homeowner as you will soon see why.

    I had the opportunity to investigate a beautiful bed and breakfast back on February 15, 2003 alongside my first official paranormal team. I remember this night vividly as I was at a special event for the release of "Daredevil" at a local theater. That night the weather was awful. It was snowing. It was sleeting. The roads were horrible, but even with all that I couldn't be kept away from the investigation. I will say that as I was leaving the theater to head out to St. Louis, I was second-guessing my decision. My normal thirty-minute commute from the theater to St. Louis took me about an hour, but I arrived safe and sound.

    The large home we were investigating was built around 1892. The owner, I'll call her Jennifer, learned there had been four deaths there. One of the deaths was the first owner of the house. He died in the large upstairs bathroom from some form of cancer. Another death was an older widow. The cause of death was unknown. Another former owner died in the library some time ago. Jennifer knows less about the fourth death, but she assured us it took place inside the mansion.

Jennifer mentioned a lot of different activity that was taking place inside the home. One of the most common occurrences is the actual appearance of a male spirit. He is believed to be the spirit of the man who died of cancer. His appearance is usually centered on the master bedroom and he appears to be completely normal until he eventually fades away. A spirit of a woman, as well as that of a child, have also been seen roaming the halls. Other things, less climatic than seeing an actual apparition, are footsteps, doors opening and closing, 1920s-era music playing and the feeling of being watched. Jennifer said activity usually picks up when they start doing renovations and as we all know, that seems to be a common trend in haunted houses.

When our group member Terry reached the house, he realized he was the first to arrive. He got a key from Jennifer before she left for a party. She told Terry that we were the only people staying that night, so we were going to have free roam of the place. Terry was in the house alone for several hours before more team members arrived. He took this time to try to get some EVP since the place was very quiet. He was able to get some sound bytes including the sound of a woman's voice.

The rest of our team eventually arrived. Terry gave us a tour of the house and we also walked around a bit to get a feel for the place. Once we got comfortable with the surroundings and heard the stories of the places of interest, we began setting up our equipment. We were pretty loaded down with what everyone brought so we hopefully were going to be able to get some great evidence. We had 35mm cameras, digital camcorders, EMF meters, motion sensors, digital sound recorders, etc. We spent quite a bit of time setting up shop. We were pretty excited about being there, so nothing was going to ruin it for us that night.

We had cameras set up in the attic, the master bedroom, the staircase, the library and the second floor hallway. We also had some voice-activated recording devices set up in various rooms. Our base of operations was in the foyer. We had our monitors set up there so we could view the cameras from a safe distance.

That night was the first for a new member named Jason. We

had him sit up on the second floor while we watched him from the monitor. Jason didn't know about the back staircase, so one of our team members crept up the back stairs and began making noises in the hallway. Jason was getting pretty creeped out. He kept telling us that something was down there. We repeatedly told him to go check it out, but he always declined. Eventually we filled him in on the prank and thankfully he found it funny as well.

As the night progressed we did witness quite a bit of activity. We had several possible orbs captured on the video cameras as well as on film. We already had the sound of a woman talking but we also got a sound clip of a person breathing very heavily. At one point in the attic, Terry captured a large black shadow move in front of the camera and then it stepped back off-camera. The interesting thing about this is none of the motion sensors were activated from this movement. We also captured a shadow on the second floor. Not a single team member was on this floor during that time. Another oddity was a little door under the stairs that kept opening while we watched the monitors. Each time someone would close it and then it would pop open again. We tried several different things to debunk it, but we never could. We tried opening doors to create a suction effect, we tried going up and down the stairs at several rates of speed and we also tried to have a lot of people go up and down the stairs to see if their weight would jar the door open. All of these were unsuccessful.

This is where the story gets a little more entertaining. Most books would have stopped at this point, but this book is about the misadventures of ghost hunting, so this part of the story is very important.

Around midnight, Jennifer returned from the party. To say she was tipsy is an understatement. She found it very difficult to make it through the door. When she got to the foyer where we were it was pretty obvious she had a fun evening. As she hobbled to our monitor she started to ask a lot of silly questions. Terry thought it'd be a great idea for her to hear one of the EVPs he acquired earlier that evening. Terry got the digital recorder and held it out in front of him at about waist level. As Jennifer tried to listen to the sound, she couldn't hear it very well, so she leaned in a little. You could see her losing her balance as she kept leaning farther and farther towards the recorder. Then, when she heard it, she got very excited. I have to say when drunken people get excited, it's pretty over the top. She threw her arms up in the air, said a couple of expletives and then she burped. That was her cue to head off to bed.

I was leaning against a desk watching everything unfold. As Jennifer started to walk past me towards the back staircase, she stumbled and fell right into the desk next to me. She assured us she was okay as she started heading down the hall again. My favorite part was as she got to the back staircase, she spun around and slurred, "Are you guys going to want breakfast in the morning?" We all looked at each other and shook our heads no. She said, "Good, I don't think I am going to feel like making it." With that last statement, up the stairs she went and we heard the bedroom door close.

We all looked at each other and started laughing. About thirty minutes passed when it hit me. I asked if anyone knew which bedroom was Jennifer's. Terry said he thought it was the master bedroom. I stated something to the effect of isn't that the bedroom where we have a video camera running? The faces of the team were priceless at this thought. Three of us went to the room and knocked on the door. Nobody answered. We knocked again and although she didn't answer the door, we heard her go into the bathroom and shut the door. Like ninjas, we slipped into the room, grabbed the camera and left. The funny thing is the camera was set up next to the bed and aimed out across the room. When we picked up the camera, Jennifer's clothes were in a pile right next to the tripod. As we got back downstairs with the camera, there was a lot of bickering over who was going to review the footage. I suggested our female team member do it. The final decision was the owner of the cam would be the one to watch it. It's actually some quite disturbing footage. To answer the question everyone is probably thinking right now, Jennifer did NOT get undressed in view of the camera. I'm not sure if she knew the camera was there or not. What the camera did film was Jennifer lying down on the bed. A few minutes later, you see her get up and head to the bathroom.

This is where the story takes a turn towards gross. The microphone picked up disembodied throwing up sounds coming from the bathroom. After a couple of minutes of that, Jennifer returned and collapsed onto the bed again. A bit later you can hear us knocking on the door. She went back to the bathroom and we rushed in to rescue the camera, thus finishing off the segment. I have to say that in all my years of ghost hunting, this was probably one of the strangest things I have ever had happen on an investigation. In the end though, with all our findings, this house definitely had some paranormal activity.

Lessons Learned

1. Do what it takes to explain any activity. If you go in with the mindset that a place is haunted, you'll have a hard time convincing yourself that it's not.

2. So many directions I can go here. I'll stick with this one: pay attention to where you set up your equipment. You never know when you may need to relocate it or when you may need to leave in a hurry.

VII. HAUNTING ALTON WITH A LITTLE TLC

I guess Troy Taylor saw something special in me because we became friends very quickly after meeting for the first time. He must have had a keen eye for "up and coming" paranormal investigators because he was quick to take me under his wing and make me somewhat of an apprentice. One of our first investigations was in Salem at the McMackin House, a quaint little restaurant in southern Illinois that had an extensive history with the paranormal. To say I was excited that Troy would consider me for this task was an understatement. I had a head the size of the Waverly Hills Sanitarium as I pranced around my house gathering up my gear. It was a very interesting night for the two of us, and by all means, if you see us in person, do ask.

Although this was a great time and I was very honored to have helped Troy with the investigation, it in no way, shape or form, compared to the next adventure I was about to partake.

In May of 2003, Troy contacted me about doing another investigation with him. This time it was going to be in Alton, Illinois, at the First Unitarian Church. Before I could even say yes, he informed me that our investigation was going to be produced by *The Learning Channel*. I played a munchkin in my fifth grade class' version of "The Wizard of Oz," so performing wasn't something new for me.

In sixth grade I took on a more demanding role as I played Ben Rogers, one of the most important people who helped Tom Sawyer paint the fence. I even had the lead in my high school musical, "Time and Time Again." Basically, this was the musical version of the movie "Back to the Future," so in short, I was no stranger to acting and this was going to be my big break. All these thoughts were going through my head as I muttered, "Three weeks from now? I'll have my people call your people." What Troy didn't realize was I was already doing the happy dance on the other end of the phone.

Our plan for the show was to be centered on the basement of the church. Proving the church to be haunted due to a former minister committing suicide was not what Troy's intentions were for the taping. Sure, a lot of the activity can be attributed to the minister's demise, but that activity is centralized around the sanctuary and the area where his office once stood. We already knew this to be true; we needed a challenge to push us to the limits of our intellect.

So, what about the basement? What could be causing the activities that are happening in that area of the church? One of the most common occurrences in the basement is that of different noises emanating throughout the building. Sounds of adults talking and singing are quite often heard, but it's also the sound of children. Sometimes happy, sometimes sad, either way a lot of emotion is still hanging around the basement of the church. The feeling that one gets while walking around in the basement seems to be more of an "uneasy" type of sensation. Perhaps fear, maybe desperation, either way we had our ideas of the cause of this phenomenon. It was Troy's belief that the church had been part of the Underground Railroad, a network of secret routes and safe houses that 19th century slaves used to escape to freedom. Of course there are no records stating it was, but that's expected since no records were kept of any involvement with this service. Our plan for the show was to possibly use history to explain what was happening in the basement of the First Unitarian Church. See what you think.

Production Day

The show we were being taped for was called "Mysterious Worlds: America's Ghost Hunters" and it was going to be aired a couple days before Halloween in 2003. The show was set to showcase several paranormal investigative teams from all over the United States. Each team specialized in a different form of investigating the paranormal. There was Troy and myself using history to help prove and explain why a place is haunted. Another team focused on EVP to record voices of the dead. A third team used a lot of high tech gadgets and a fourth team actually trained a dog to sniff out spirits. I can't help but think of the Sesame Street song, "One of These Things Is Not Like the Other" when I see this lineup. Well, three out of four isn't too bad I suppose.

I had to leave work early that day to get to Alton in time for the investigation. Actually I left a lot early, but I wanted to make sure I didn't miss anything. Since I had some time to kill before the actual investigation was going to start, I spoke with the church secretary to hear some history and stories about the building. Although I had been to the church and I knew a lot about it from speaking with Troy and hearing his stories on the Alton Ghost Tours, it was still very interesting to get the opinion of someone who actually worked at the church. I must say I felt a little awkward at first. Most church employees don't like to talk about their house of worship being haunted. At least that's how it is in the states. Countries like England seem to be a little more open to discussing paranormal activities within a church's walls. The secretary began telling me stories of hearing noises coming from the sanctuary. Sounds of music playing, people singing, and other types of sounds would be heard at all times. When nighttime rolled around, it was very rare for anyone associated with the church to stay there after dark. If one person were to leave, everyone would leave because they wouldn't want to be left there alone. The secretary expressed a sincere discomfort with some of the things going on around the church and oddly enough, it comforted me to have a chance to witness these things first hand. After speaking with the secretary for about thirty minutes, Troy and the production crew began showing up.

Now just to let you know, I was dressed for success. I had on my nicest pair of jeans and a button-up dress shirt. I was having a good hair day, and my beard was nicely trimmed. Troy came wearing his usual jean shorts and denim shirt. For those of us who know Troy, I am convinced either he has his own denim clothing line, or he owns stock in Levi Strauss. Either way, I was about to be on TV!

We began the day with shooting the outside the church. The usual weird angles and close ups and zoom outs (if that's what they are called) that the production companies like to use as filler were filmed right away. I was getting concerned at this time because I hadn't really been on camera yet, but that was about to change. Well, kind of. We started to film some more filler material. First was a shot of Troy and me walking down the sidewalk in front of the church, followed by a shot of us walking up the stairs, and finally through the front door. Although I was happy to be on camera at this point, I'm pretty sure my "behind" isn't my best feature.

Once inside the building, we met up with Peg Flach. She was a historian who also experienced many strange happenings in the church. She, too, was to be used for the taping of this show. At first I saw her as competition for the camera, but that was short-lived once one of the production guys started filling me in on my role for the show.

My understanding of the investigation was that we were doing just that, investigating the church. What area or to what extent of investigating we were doing was beyond me. It wasn't until I was informed that I would be wearing a hat camera that I realized we may be investigating uncharted ground. The only uncharted ground I knew of in the church was the actual crawlspace. All of a sudden me dressing up for my "big break" was about to be a bad move because we were going to be getting dirty. But what the heck, the show must go on.

Once Troy got back from taping some segments with Peg, we started to gather our gear for the investigative part of the show. I was armed with a hat camera and a thermal scanner, Troy was armed merely with his digital camera and we both had flashlights. Not to sound too obvious, but a hat camera is a camera attached to the bill of a hat. It had a wire that came down behind my ear and ran under my shirt and into a hip pack.

Inside the hip pack was a recording device that would tape the images captured by the camera. This camera was equipped with infrared so it would be able to record images in complete darkness. The thermal scanner is a device that can record temperatures in an area using infrared light. Above all the fancy tools we had, we were also armed with five other very important pieces to any paranormal investigation toolbox: our senses.

As we approached the area where we were going to climb up into the crawlspace, I realized that we were about to crawl through dirt, rust, nails and most likely asbestos. I felt pretty stupid at this point due to my choice of wardrobe. Those feelings were quickly remedied by Troy when I realized that he had his usual shorts on. Of course Troy is the expert in this field and within minutes changed into a pair of pants at the bookstore, located only a few blocks away. That's Troy Taylor, always teaching me new things within the paranormal field.

A view of where we climbed up into the crawlspace beneath the church

Lesson learned: always, always bring an extra pair of pants, not only in case of getting dirty, but also in case of soiling your pants out of pure fright.

Once we got into the crawlspace, it wasn't too bad. This may come to a surprise to some, but I think this area is called a crawlspace because we actually had to crawl to get through it. There was an eerie feeling attached to this area and within seconds I witnessed the largest orb I had ever seen in my life. I want to paint the picture for you as best as I can. Imagine if you will, Troy crawling in front of me as we make our way under the church. I am crawling right behind Troy, sticking close to him, not because I was scared, but just to make sure Troy was going to be okay in this scary setting. The camera on my hat was aiming straight ahead as I crawled through the rubble. The orb I captured was none other than Troy Taylor's backside. He must have been working out prior to the investigation because it was a perfectly shaped orb. What's more, it was so bright, that while we crawled I tried not to make eye contact in order to protect myself from falling into its spell.

All joking aside, about halfway back through the crawlspace, Troy's digital camera went dead. The fully charged batteries were completely zapped of any life they had. I remember Troy's reaction to this was much like that of a kid who had his favorite toy broken in front of him by his older brother. This wasn't the only thing to go wrong while were investigating the crawlspace. I'll get to that in a bit.

Digital camera or not, we had to press on. After crawling for what seemed like forever, we reached the back of the church. It was at this moment that we actually found something worthy of mention. In the far back corner of the crawlspace, we found an entrance to a little room. It would be my estimate that this room was approximately ten feet by ten feet with a height of around 48 inches. It seemed large enough for a person to crawl through the opening and sit comfortably. The room may have been bigger at one time. The debris under the church seemed pretty thick and it appeared to even clog up the doorway to the room. Once we found this room, we looked around, recorded some video and made our way back to the area where we entered the crawlspace. Oddly enough, although I was covered entirely in dirt and grime, a simple dusting off and my clothes became spotless.

I wish I could say the same for my nose. I was still blowing dirt out of my nose when this show aired on TV in October, and we taped it in May.

If you have been reading my story word for word, (what do you mean you've been skimming?) you would have read where I mentioned something else happening after Troy's camera went dead. When we got our feet back on the basement floor and we were finally able to stand in the upright position, the production crew wanted to see the hat camera footage of the hidden room. Strangely, upon reviewing the tape, it actually stopped recording shortly after Troy's camera died. I was very upset at this because here we were, crawling through this rough terrain to find evidence that this was part of the Underground Railroad, and when we did find it, the camera didn't record the footage. Immediately, I told them to hook me up with another tape and batteries and we could crawl back in and try again. They actually said not to worry about it, they could make do with what footage we had. I was surprised by this. What better way to prove our theory than to find a hidden room to justify the thought process. After a few minutes of going back and forth, they finally gave in and set me up for another go at recording the room. Bad move on my part.

Now, when it comes to my investigative team, I am commonly known as "the bait" and/or "the meat" and sometimes just plain and simply "the rat." This is due to me always being the first to go into dark areas. Sometimes I am the one who also gets shoved in to the small cramped doorways leading to who-knows-what. I am not really sure how I got this distinction because I am six feet tall and I weigh about 190, but that's part of the job. I don't mind doing it, because if there's treasure on the other side, I get first crack at it.

This time when they set me up with the new tape and batteries, I carried only the essentials. I had the hat cam on along with the hip pack, and I had a little flashlight in my mouth. I climbed up into the crawlspace yet again. When I got everything in place to journey through the twists and turns, I asked if anyone was going to join me. No one answered me. Everyone had left and gone back to the sanctuary to record more footage. So now I was in a dark, haunted basement, in an area where if I did get scared by a ghost, I couldn't even run away crying. My only chance would have been to either crawl away or lie there in the fetal position until help arrived. Unfortunately, I was about to undergo this task all by myself.

I will admit I was a little scared about this. I knew all the stories about the basement and I had seen enough scary movies to know that you never go into confined places alone. I can honestly say I had never crawled so fast in my life. If speed crawling were an art, my technique would have been considered masterful. I compare it to that of a cat in a litter box kind of movement. I was flinging dirt behind me as I made my way to the little room yet again. Once back there, I removed the camera from my hat, checked the recorder to make sure it was still working and I actually put the cam into the room to better show the dimensions. Once I felt like I acquired enough footage to adequately prove our theory (about five or six seconds because I got scared,) I made my way back into the basement. I dusted off, wiped off my scared expression and went back upstairs like it was nothing to be down there by myself. They had just finished filming and were getting ready to call it a day, thus ending my first televised investigation.

So to answer the questions about the room and the possibility of the church being associated with the Underground Railroad. Here are a few things to take in consideration as you make your judgment. This room actually falls outside of the church's foundation. Not only does it fall outside of the original foundation, it isn't even listed on the floor plans for the church. If you consider the difficulty required to get back to this room, it seems very strange that a church would require such a hidden location. Did I say hidden location? Also known as a location to hide things? Would the church need to hide Bibles, hymnals or candles? Perhaps, but most likely, it was probably used to hide more precious things such as human beings. It would also explain why the sounds of people singing emanate from the basement. Slaves would often find comfort by singing as it would give them hope for a better tomorrow.

The whole experience of this day will last me a lifetime. I told everyone I knew that I was going to be on TV, and if they didn't watch it, I would disown them. Now Len Adams has expressed some jealousy because of Troy selecting me over him, which is understandable. Len is much better looking than I am, and Troy wanted to be the center of attention for the program. The camera loves Len, as do the cold spots.

This day in my life was also a continuation of Troy following me wherever I went. When I went to Adams, Tennessee for the Bell Witch Festival, Troy followed me. When I went to Louisville, Kentucky to see Waverly Hills Sanatorium, Troy followed me. In fact, he also followed me the second time I went there just recently. When I went up to Decatur to the Lincoln Theater, Troy was right behind me. I've been teaching him everything I know, even when it comes to giving tours.

Lessons Learned

1. Be dressed for the investigation - Be mindful of your shirt, pants and shoes. Outdoor and indoor venues require different attire as do above ground and underground investigations.

2. Don't follow Troy so closely when crawling behind him.

VIII. DING DONG --- THE BELL WITCH IS NEVER DEAD!

Most people in the paranormal world are familiar with the story of the Bell Witch. This is actually one of my favorite stories of all time. Many of my co-workers and friends have been a victim of my telling of this story. It's such an incredible tale that that has plenty of drama, suspense, horror and terror! As there are books out there where you can read about the Bell Witch in great detail, I am only including a brief history to set up the story. After that, I will go into my experience down in Adams, Tennessee.

History of the Bell Witch

The story of the Bell Witch took place back in 1817. John Bell moved to Tennessee in the early 1800s, but it was in 1817 that things started to go awry at the Bell farm. There are several different accounts as to what stirred up the paranormal activity on the farm. One version is that Bell shot at a strange animal he saw in his field one night, which sparked the torment he would later receive. A second version is that one of his sons found an Indian skull and brought it back to the house. While examining the skull, one of the teeth became dislodged and it fell between the floorboards. The idea behind this story is that the paranormal activity was centered on that tooth not being returned to the Indian's burial place. Yet a third version leads us to believe that a neighboring woman with whom John Bell had a dispute was actually a witch. During a court trial between Bell and Kate Batts, Kate was said to have put a curse on the Bell family, which sparked the activity at the farm. These are only a few explanations for what caused the phenomenon, however no one knows for sure why it happened. On the other hand, we do know that this was, in fact, happening to the Bell family. The entity was deemed a witch because during that time, people believed witches existed and they were terrified of them.

Initially, there were knocks on the doors, windows and walls of the Bell cabin. Each time the family heard these noises, they'd rush out onto the porch and would find nothing. The haunting eventually really started to pester the family. While they were sleeping, an unseen hand would pull the covers off the beds. It would pull the children's hair and often times physically assault them. The Bell Witch especially harassed John's daughter, Betsy. The girl would have her hair tied in a knot; she'd get slapped and dragged about by her hair. John also was abused severely by the spirit.

During the early stages of the spirit's existence, the family would be able to hear a faint voice. Often times this voice would just be mumbling, but there were times where the listener could make out the spirit singing a hymn. As time passed, the witch became stronger and she would be heard very clearly and loudly by anyone present on the farm. The witch would hold conversations with the Bells, she'd recite sermons by various local preachers and she'd even spread gossip about people in town.

No matter what the family did, it always seemed the witch was present. She'd follow them around when they left the house, tormenting and teasing them constantly. Stories say that she would be very kind to John Bell's wife, Lucy. Sometimes the witch would leave a fresh baked pie on the windowsill for Lucy. The witch seemed to interact with the family in different ways. She abused John and Betsy and she helped Lucy around the kitchen. Stories say that one night, as John Jr. was watching his sister and father get abused, he lashed out at the witch, telling her to leave his family alone and take him on. The witch said something to the effect of, "I can do you no more harm than to have you watch your family suffer." And that's what the witch did, day in and day out.

The story also tells how Andrew Jackson heard of the stories going around about the haunting. John Jr. and Jesse (another Bell son) both fought under Jackson at the Battle of New Orleans. Old Hickory set out to visit the family and find out what was going on. As his entourage approached the farm, their wagon abruptly stopped. The horses and the men were unable to get it to budge. The witch spoke up and told the group to continue their journey and she'd see them that night. Instantly, the wagon was able to move. As Jackson got to the farm, one of his men was attacked by the witch, who promised to point out a fraud among the group the next day. After hours of pleading with the witch, Andrew Jackson and his men left the next morning. As we all know, Jackson became the President of the United States years later. He wrote about his visit to the Bell family in his memoirs.

Eventually around 1820, John Bell passed away. Near his deathbed, a bottle of poison was discovered. The witch spoke to the family, telling them that she had poisoned John the night before and began laughing hysterically. The surviving Bells eventually moved away, but the people of Adams will tell you that the witch's spirit still remains at the Bell family farm.

I was very excited to see that a movie was coming out to tell this story. For those of you who haven't seen it, it's called *An American Haunting.* Unfortunately, Hollywood used one of the other explanations of what caused the haunting. I will not go into detail as I do not want to ruin anything for you if you haven't seen it. To me, it seemed like more of a Hollywood controversial type of reasoning. When the story unfolded and I saw where they were going with it, my jaw just dropped. I looked at my wife and she had the same reaction. In my opinion I thought the movie was done well. It seemed to really capture the essence of the times and the torment that this family had to suffer through. By all means watch the movie, but if you'd like a more true account, read Troy Taylor's book *Season of the Witch*. It is, in my opinion, one of his best works!

Bell Witch? Bring it!

Several years ago, I had the opportunity to head down to Adams, Tenn., to witness firsthand the location of the Bell With phenomenon. There was to be an actual Bell Witch Festival taking place during the weekend. This was an event that I was even able to get my wife to come to. Along with our van driver Randy, his wife, Sharon, and a couple of other passengers, Mandy and Rex, we set out to what we hoped would be an incredible experience.

Upon arriving at the event, it seemed as though we were the only ones there. We walked around the grounds for a bit trying to locate someone to talk to, but the people we did find were all asleep in their vehicles. Mind you, we were a bit early. However, it didn't appear that much was done to set up for the festival, so perhaps they should have been there early as well.

Finally, after about 30 minutes of walking around aimlessly, we ran into a familiar face. Lo and behold, Troy Taylor, in all his glory, was walking toward the park grounds! Alongside Troy was a good friend and author Dave Goodwin. We caught up with them and they looked just as lost as we were. Troy was very involved with the event, not as an organizer, but as a presenter, and he seemed clueless and not very happy with the lack of organization. Troy and Dave were going to have a booth where they would sell some of Troy's books, but they couldn't begin setting up without any direction of where to go. If I remember correctly, Troy uttered a few expletives and began setting up wherever he wanted to. All the other vendors who came after Troy began setting up near him as well.

Once the event started, there was more chaos. It seemed like people didn't know where they were to check in. There wasn't a whole lot of fun stuff going on at this point. The morning consisted of people walking around, looking at buildings, watching the clouds, etc. Eventually, the speakers would start their presentations, and then all would be wonderful in the world. At least that was what I hoped.

There was no way to know when someone was going to be speaking since there were no schedules. Troy tells this story best, and I will try to capture a bit of his essence.

A little into the afternoon I decided to find out when I was going to need to speak to the festival attendees. I walked up to the organizer to ask him for a schedule or to find out when he needed me to speak. The guy looked around a minute, asked me what time it was now, and then said, "Well, when do YOU want to speak?"

This is just a small sample of how unorganized the presentations were. I would sometimes just come randomly come across a person speaking from the back of a building. There weren't even chairs for the spectators. I remember vividly sitting on the grass as various insects made me their playground. This was very unfortunate as there were several speakers that I wanted to hear in person, but couldn't, due to not knowing when they would be speaking.

Nothing exciting happened the rest of the day and I began questioning my decision to come. Heather and I had paid quite a bit of money to be able to attend the event and I definitely didn't feel I was getting my value. We ended up going back to the hotel and watching TV until the night events were about to start.

Unfortunately, I didn't sign up for any of the events that were to be held after hours. Troy told me I could probably talk to someone and pay to get admitted to the event before it started. Rex and Mandy were signed up, so Heather and I rode along to drop them off at the Red River Campground. I walked around until I found somebody to speak to about joining the overnight event. I gave him fifty dollars and he proceeded to put it in his pocket. I wasn't sure if the money ever made it to the right person, but no bother; it was not my problem now.

The schedule was as follows: we were going to start out from the campground. From there, we were to take a bus to an old farm where we'd be loaded onto wagons. We'd take the hayride out to the old Clark Mill location where we would conjure up the spirits with an actual séance! After that, we were going to head back to the farm, get back on the bus and then arrive safely (I wasn't so sure) back at the campground. I had a feeling that this was going to be an interesting adventure.

Sadly, I was the first person to actually step onto the bus. I hope I don't offend any "bus rights activists" when I say that ancient vehicle should have been put out of its misery a long time ago. When I started to walk down the aisle, I discovered I was walking through years of spider webs. Every web seemed to get me in the eye or the mouth and I began flailing my arms as I tried to get them off me. I am sure I looked really creepy to the people waiting to get on the bus. However weird I looked, the people who got on after me would be walking into a de-spider-webbed bus due to my frantic efforts of web removal.

The webs weren't the only upsetting aspect about the bus. Due to my history of riding buses to school, I realized the importance of sitting in the back. Even at my age, I still need to show people how cool I am and nothing is cooler than the back of the bus. Once I got to my seat, I noticed a lot of the windows in the bus were open. I noticed piles of leaves and dust and other debris resting on the seats. In the back corner there was even a bird's nest. I had the strangest feeling that this bus hadn't been used in quite awhile. It was very entertaining to watch people's faces as they tried to find a seat. Even more fun was to see people with white pants sit down. Ahhh, good times. Good times.

We probably sat on that bus for about 30 minutes before the driver arrived. Everyone was gearing to go. Everyone, that is, except the bus. It just didn't feel like starting that night. About five minutes later, the engine finally turned over and we were about to head out to the farm. It was at this moment that everyone was overcome with gas fumes from the bus' exhaust. After breathing this in for the fifteen-minute ride, we were sure to see apparitions due to the high we were all experiencing. I don't remember for sure, as I suspect I blacked out briefly, but I think saw the Bell Witch fly over our bus during the ride. Don't quote me on that one, though.

When we arrived at the farm I began to feel a little better about the night. We were rounded up and loaded onto two hay wagons. It was fun watching people getting creeped out during the excursion. There was absolutely nothing scary about it. We were in the middle of a field on an old grass road. At least they were having a good time, which was more than I could have said about my day.

We headed back to the site of the Clark Mill, which has a story relating to the Bell Witch. Everyone walked around a bit as we waited for the other wagon to arrive. The area was pretty neat. You couldn't see the mill; I'm not sure where it was or even if it still existed. There were trees all around and you could hear a stream flowing within the wooded area. Once we were all in place, we formed a circle and the séance was about to begin.

I've always wanted to be part of a séance, so I was very excited about this opportunity. Just so the day would remain consistent, this was quite the letdown as well. I don't want to mention any names, as I don't want to offend anyone, but I'll break it down for the readers.

We were all put into a large circle. There were probably about fifty people in the group, so it was more of an oval with a couple of corners since it's too hard to organize that many people into an actual geometrically correct shape. We were then instructed to hold hands and form a chain that wouldn't be broken by the spirits. Our guide then lit some candles and did a few rituals to open her up to the spirits. Then she told us she was going to place sage on our foreheads to protect us from any evil spirits. She began to look through her bag, which was placed in the center of our human circle. After searching for a couple of minutes, I could tell she was getting a little concerned. Her friend came over to her to see what the issue was. They whispered to each other for a bit and then the friend began searching the bag. I couldn't help but laugh to myself. I had the feeling that they forgot the sage. Sure enough, our guide stood up and announced, "I forgot the sage!" She said she had a substitute in her bag so it wasn't a big deal. To me it was, though. I wasn't sure about this séance thing, and if we are supposed to have sage, then I wanted sage! The woman then reached down into her bag and pulled out some other substance that was going to protect us from the evil spirits just the same as sage would. I think to calm down the concerns some people may have had, she figured putting anything on our foreheads would have been better than nothing. When she placed the substance on my forehead, it smelled like Dial dish soap to me.

Either way, I was safe from the bad spirits and leftover grease stains because of it.

As we stood in the oblong circle, the séance conductor began to explain some of things we might experience during the session. She said we might hear the sound of people walking through the grass behind us. We may also feel the sensation of someone standing directly behind us, as if they were waiting to come into our circle. It may get cold, we may get lightheaded, we may start crying, etc. It honestly felt like one of the pharmaceutical commercials where they give you the list of twenty possible side-effects if you take a certain kind of medicine.

Eventually, the séance began and I was just hanging on for the ride. I do have to say that I had a very eerie feeling during the process. There wasn't any wind that night but it did sound as if something was moving through the trees. There was also one point, which lasted quite awhile, where it sounded as if the stream began splashing about. It could have possibly been a deer or some other animal running through the water. No matter what it was, it was very unsettling. The splashing water was very loud and only occurred during the actual séance. That was a strange thing to experience.

As we got further into the séance, one girl began to have some kind of vision. She started crying and began to paint a picture of what she was seeing. She described a little girl with curly hair and a flowered dress. She said the little girl was scared and was running from something. Could it be? Was this girl actually seeing Betsy Bell? Was Betsy scared of the entity that had tormented her family for so long? The suspense at this point was to die for! The girl went on with her vision and confirmed that it was indeed Betsy (which proved to me that she knew the story quite well.) She wept quite a bit during this performance, as she described more details of her vision.

As if this wasn't enough for us, she then proceeded to get us involved. She asked that all of us picture this little girl in our minds. The girl - we'll go with the story so let's call her Betsy - was trying to run to a lighted doorway but something was keeping her back. For this effect we had to imagine a rope tied to this girl's waist holding her at bay. But how could we help this girl? Her advancement to the door was hindered by an imaginary rope. Well, we did what anybody would do in a situation like this. We pictured a giant pair of scissors cutting the rope, thus setting Betsy free to run to the light. Just then, a couple of other girls started crying. I started laughing to myself. It just seemed all too fake and premeditated for me to take seriously. Perhaps it was planned out by the person who began speaking of her vision, and the other girls just got caught up in the emotion. If so, I apologize if they are reading about my laughing at the whole scenario.

The séance ended shortly after that. In fact, it ended quite abruptly. This may have been because snacks and drinks were provided and people were probably hungry. It seemed odd that we went through all this stuff to open the séance, but did nothing to close it. Did that mean the evil spirits were possibly still outside the scattered remnants of our circle?

As people began stuffing down the food, I wandered around on my own. I am actually very glad that I did. I wandered over to the trees where I had heard the water splashing about. The water had calmed down at this point and all I could hear was just the subtle flow of a little spring. I stepped back from the trees and took some pictures. Two other people came over by me and stood looking at the trees with me. I asked them if they had noticed a change in how the water sounded during the séance. They agreed and we headed back to the group. It wasn't until I got home and developed the film that I saw what I had captured.

Everybody was loaded back onto the wagons and we began heading back to the farm. I did have an interesting debate with a guy on the ride back. His theory was that after a certain amount of time, hauntings cease to exist in a set location. Not meaning that ghosts will no longer inhabit the world, but more like they have an actual life expectancy that dissipates over the years. I, of course, disagreed with him. I began to throw out examples of European ghost lore that have been around for hundreds of years. These hauntings are still going on to this day. He disagreed with me a little more until I eventually threw some hay in his eyes and booted him off the wagon. I still don't know if he found his way out of the field or not. All I know is my ride back to the farm was quieter because everyone was scared of me. Of course I am kidding about the results of the discussion, but the debate did happen. It's an interesting theory for you to

The first photo I took, take note of the tree on the left

The second photo I took. There appears to be ectoplasm in the photo. The tree is still seen on the left side showing that the photos were taken in the same location.

ponder on your own time.

We got back to the bus, went through a few minutes of trying to get it started and eventually made it back to the campground. There was another event scheduled for that night. I didn't take part in it, thankfully. I headed my sleepy butt back to the hotel. Participants in the event I passed up were going to be spending the night in the "actual" Bell family cabin! Sounds spooky! In fact, they would be staying in a "replica cabin." The real cabin doesn't exist anymore. Even sillier than the way it was billed, is the replica cabin isn't even located in the area of the original Bell family farm. Mandy and Rex were involved in this overnight and said that nobody knew what was going on. People who were put in charge of the event had no idea what they were supposed to be doing. The guy running things was making out with some girl from the festival. Within a couple of hours, everyone had pretty well given up on this ghostly adventure and gone back to their homes or hotels.

A replica of the Bell Family Cabin - spooky huh?

Then came the next day, which was sure to come with its own share of adventures. I ended up sleeping in that morning while Randy, Sharon and Heather spent some time in Clarksville, Tennessee. That seemed to be the highlight of my wife's trip! For me, I was still waiting for an opportunity to get excited. I was going to be involved in an old fashioned all-you-can-eat Southern barbeque taking place at the campground later that evening. Dinner can be exciting and, as you'll soon see, it didn't let us down.

I honestly don't remember much about the day in general. It seemed very much like the previous unorganized day. I listened to a few speakers, I annoyed Troy by spending time at his booth, and I walked around the museum and ate some lunch. I really wanted to go into the Bell Witch Cave, but it was closed due to some recent flooding. That was a major letdown. The whole time I was down there, the idea of going into the cave was my saving grace. Talk about devastation. I nearly ripped the closed sign off the gate! The only thing I was looking forward to at this point was the barbeque dinner, and it didn't come soon enough.

I was dropped off at the campground and waited around until Troy, Dave and the others arrived. Yet again, things seemed to be unorganized (a common trend that weekend.) Nobody knew where to sit. The picnic tables were filthy. There was going to be a special presentation on the Bell Witch by some experts as well as a panel discussion with some of the speakers. As long as the food was there, I didn't think this could get messed up, but I of course was wrong.

While Troy, Dave and I waited for the food to be ready, one of the coordinators came over to our table. He said the special presenter cancelled and he needed to Troy to help him (I like to call it "bailing him out.") Troy was not prepared for this at all. As those of you who have heard Troy speak before, he doesn't need much preparation. He can go for hours and hours and hours. Although Troy was reluctant, he did agree to help.

When the food was finally ready, we rushed up to the little outhouse building they served the food from. I think we only knocked over a couple of elderly people on the way, but hey, you snooze you lose. When we go to the building I couldn't believe the spread. The all-you-can-eat Southern barbeque consisted of a bucket of barbecued beef slopped onto a little bun. We also got corn, a little salad and a roll. This is when something really funny happened. As Troy, Dave and I all got back to the table, we decided to all sit on the same side. The picnic table started to flip over but we very quickly caught it. And just like a falling drunk man and his beer, nothing spilled! Well I am Polish, but I still don't know how the others justified their decision to sit on the same side of the table.

I was probably one of the first five people to go up for seconds. I couldn't believe it when the guy said, "I think we have enough for one more sandwich." This was supposed to be an "all-you-can-eat" feast. Not an "all-you-can-eat-as-long-as-it's-not-more-than-we-have-available" type of meal. There was also dessert, which was a little cup of ice cream. The night wasn't starting off too well for me yet again.

During Troy's impromptu presentation on the Bell Witch, I was blown away by how good he is when he's unprepared. He truly was an expert on the story and he kept us very entertained. After Troy's presentation, they brought a couple of other speakers up to do a panel discussion. This was okay, nothing too exciting. It was fun to watch Troy's face as the topics of psychics and UFOs were brought up. He seemed to not have much to say about those topics. So if you ever want to shut Troy up, just tell him you were abducted by aliens once while in a psychic trance.

The following morning we all packed up, said our goodbyes and headed back home. All and all, I'd still like to go back sometime. I felt empty inside since I was unable to venture into the Bell Witch cave. I am sure I'll have an opportunity soon enough as the cave won't be going anywhere.

Lessons Learned

1. When running a paranormal conference - be organized. People pay good money for a positive experience.

2. When conducting a séance, have backup sage in case of an emergency.

IX. BELLEVILLE, ILLINOIS HISTORIC HOME

A couple of years ago I had the opportunity to visit a home with Len Adams. It was located in the beautiful historic district of Belleville, Illinois. Growing up in Illinois made me familiar with the area and even as a child it creeped me out. Now, as an adult, I was going to have the opportunity of investigating a house in Belleville -- the same area that had unnerved me for years.

Len and I went there one afternoon and did an initial interview with the homeowner. I'll call her Mary. She gave us a tour of the huge house and we eventually ended up in the kitchen to proceed with the interview. Despite the house's large size, the household consisted of Mary and her youngest daughter. It was very hard to believe how they could maintain this home with just the two of them. We later found out the house was for sale due to that very reason. The upkeep and bills were just too much for the small family.

As we were sitting in the kitchen asking questions, I had a very strange occurrence happen. The kitchen was a normal kitchen with all the usual fixings. There was a nice breakfast bar with tall stools in the center of the room where we were stationed for the interview. Len and I sat on the stools with our backs to the dining room area. The entrance to the dining room from the kitchen had large double doors that slid into the wall on both sides. They were open about five or six inches. As we sat there asking questions and getting to know the homeowner, I turned my head to the left towards Len. As I watched him speak (I'm not sure why, I see it all the time because he never shuts up,) out of the corner of my eye I saw movement. I looked at the double doors just in time to see a little girl, with curly blonde hair and a red dress, walk past the opening. She would have been moving across the dining room toward the hallway when I saw her. It was only for a second, as the door wasn't opened very much. I didn't say anything but kept watching the kitchen door that led to the hallway. After waiting for someone come into the kitchen, I asked Mary if her daughter was home. She said no, her daughter was gone for the day. That's when I realized what I had just seen and I began to tell Len and Mary. She didn't act surprised as they see a little girl there quite frequently. Other activity involved footsteps, doors opening and closing as well as a frequent banging noise coming from the attic.

After visiting for an hour or so, it was time to leave. We were soon going to come back with our team. Len and I were very excited with the possibility of activity in this home. We already had one experience so we were hopeful it wasn't going to be our last. Several weeks later, we were back.

I had to work that night so I didn't get there until after everyone else did. Unfortunately, as I pulled up to the house, it was like pulling into a Wal-Mart parking lot. The driveway was packed with vehicles and I only recognized a couple of them as belonging to team members. When I stepped into the dining room, there were eight or ten people sitting or standing around. It was Len, Julie, Bill and I from our team. Then it was Mary, her boyfriend, Mary's oldest daughter and her three friends. There may have been more, all I know is I was really caught off guard to see that many people looking at me when I walked in.

Although we prefer to have smaller numbers, I decided to

make the best of it. I was just hoping that with all our energy, perhaps something would happen for us. We did introductions and proceeded to get our equipment ready for the night. I was packing a little light that evening, for which I am glad since most equipment was useless with that many people. I had my digital camera, my thermal scanner and a video camera ready to go. I set the video camera up in the hallway near the staircase and the other equipment was with me as I walked around.

Initially we all stayed in the dining room to try to conjure up some activity. We were unable to get anything paranormal to happen and we eventually divided up into groups to search the house. This time, we were able to control things a little better. Mary and her boyfriend went upstairs to bed. Some of us investigated the basement while others stayed in the dining room area. Since Mary and her boyfriend were up there, we avoided the upstairs area. We figured we would try to come back later under better conditions and investigate the upstairs then.

It seems the only thing that happened that night involved the dining room area. Len placed his Tri-Field EMF detector in the center of the dining room table. For those of you who unfamiliar with EMF, it stands for Electromagnetic Field. Paranormal researchers believe that spikes in EMF can indicate paranormal activity. I agree with this theory, however I also feel that one needs another source of evidence even when the EMF detector begins squealing. So if you hear the detector's alarm, start taking photos and see if you can get something captured. That way, you have two sources of paranormal activity from two separate data collectors.

What happened that night was very strange because when we set the detector on the table, everyone left the room and the doors were shut. The detector was sitting in there for hours with not a single peep coming from it. Then all of a sudden, it started going crazy. Len and I were downstairs with a couple of people just exploring when Julie called us on the walkie-talkies. She said the Tri-Field meter had been going off for about five minutes and wouldn't stop. Len and I came upstairs and sure enough, it was singing to us. We just stood there and listened for a minutes when Len finally said he'd make it stop. He walked to the doors, opened them up and stepped inside. As if on cue, the meter stopped and sat silent. Len then checked the device and replaced the batteries. Everything seemed fine, so he set it back down and stepped outside. Within five minutes it started to sing again. This was truly a strange moment for the eight of us in attendance.

Eventually, Mary came downstairs to see what that noise was. She decided to step into the dining room to speak to the spirit, but she was met with the activity stopping and everything went back to normal. The rest of the night seemed to be more of a comedy show as we began telling stories. We knew we weren't going to be able to do much more since it was getting late and there was just so much activity from everyone there. We called it a night and headed home to start reviewing footage. Nobody got anything strange on any of our recording equipment. But based on how the EMF detector acted, we knew we wanted to come back. A month later, we did.

The house was still for sale, so there was a bit of urgency. The family had already moved out, so we had the place to ourselves. Of course, with no family there, it also meant no running water or heat. There was, however, electricity, which comes into play later. During this investigation, it was Len, Kim, Len's son Josh and his girlfriend Andrea, Julie, Matt and I. It was only our team members and nobody else. We spent some time at first in the dining room area. Len set up his camera on us and we just sat there trying to talk to the spirits.

Any chances of cold spots were thrown out the window because the entire house was a cold spot. I sat there at the table looking like a cross between the professional poker player Phil "The Unibomber" Laak and Kenny from South Park. I had my hooded sweatshirt covering my entire head and face, revealing only my eyes. I couldn't believe how cold it was in that house. We were all tired, cold and slaphappy that evening. To be honest with you, it seemed that if we laughed hard, things would start to happen. The entire time we sat there, nothing happened until we began having fun. Perhaps our laughter was giving the spirits energy to manifest or maybe they were making themselves known so they could be part of the fun. Either way, Len began to capture several orbs on his video camera. Although we try to be very professional when we do investigations, a little fun never hurt anyone. In this case, a little laughter and joking around helped stir up some of the activity.

After spending about an hour in the dining room we decided to split up and explore the building. My job was to investigate the attic. Since I am considered "the bait," I was already used to this type of assignment. To get to the attic, you had to go to the second floor and walk out a door onto an outside balcony. There was a wooden staircase that led to the attic door. I took Matt and Josh with me just for witnesses, in case something happened. As I climbed up the stairs and pushed the attic door upward, I had the surprise of my life. I had my first-ever shower of real life bat droppings. It came down at such a rate that it sounded like sleet hitting the steps below. I'm not sure, but I may have had my mouth open. I scurried down the staircase towards the two laughing guys I brought with me for support. As I flailed my arms in all directions, they kept jumping away from me. I didn't have my hood up when I climbed the stairs, so it acted like a bowl and caught a lot of the droppings. As I shook about, I got most of the guano off me, but it was still trapped in my hood. Carefully, I removed the hoodie and dumped the droppings over the railing onto the ground. Then, since I am Polish, I went back up the ladder again. This time, I was more careful when opening the door. Nothing fell on me and I was able to look around the attic from the safety of the staircase. I saw about three inches of bat guano all over the attic as well as a few deceased pigeons. That was enough investigating of the attic for one night. One would suspect that the noises the family had heard were either bats or pigeons flying around the limited attic space.

Matt, Josh and I made our way back into the bedroom area and met up with everyone else. At this point something came over me that I was hoping to avoid that night. I had to use the little boy's room. Since there was no running water in the house, it became apparent that I would be using a tree. Everyone else decided to go outside with me, not to watch, but to take some pictures. Okay, that sounds bad, too. I was going to go one way; they'd go the other way and take pictures of the house. When I finished and reached the front of the house, we began to chat a little and were all looking at the home. Suddenly, a lamp turned on in the upstairs bedroom! I was glad I had already gone to the bathroom because I would have gone again when this happened. We all rushed inside and yes indeed, the light was on. We were all excited because we ALL saw it! Unfortunately as quick as we got excited, we were just as quickly devastated. Kim discovered that the lamp was on a timer. I am not sure what the odds would have been for us to all be standing in front of the house just as that light came on, but it was incredible timing to say the least. The rest of the night our mood was very somber.

Eventually it was time to pack up and we all headed home for the evening. Upon reviewing my recording devices, I came up empty again. If it wasn't for what I saw during the initial interview, I'd be hard pressed to say the home was haunted. But I know what I saw and I can't explain it. To be honest, I think this case isn't closed yet. Perhaps we'll get back in another time and maybe then we'll have more answers.

Lessons Learned:

1. Enjoy yourself and be open to having fun on an investigation. If you take things too seriously in this field, you won't last long at all.

2. Next time, Len goes in the attic first.

X. WAVERLY HILLS SANATORIUM LOUISVILLE, KENTUCKY

The greatest ghostly adventures I have ever been on would have to be my trips to Waverly Hills! A few years back, a group of us went down to a conference being held at the sanatorium. Speakers from all over the country were going to present and the night was to end with an overnight investigation of the very haunted Waverly Hills Sanatorium. We knew this was going to be an incredible experience! The building and the Louisville Ghost Hunting Society didn't let us down.

History

Waverly Hills was originally built in Louisville, Ky., in 1910. However, with the amount of patients coming into the small hospital, more space was needed. By the year 1924, a new, much larger facility was going to be constructed. Within two years, the doors officially opened. Waverly Hills was widely known as one of the top tuberculosis treatment centers in the entire country. During the early years of TB, the only known cure was fresh air and plenty of food and rest. Other attempts at cures were done as well. This often involved "experiments" on patients. Most of the time, this proved to be more painful than the TB itself. Some procedures involved finding ways to let the lungs expand freely by removing other parts of the human anatomy. Ribs were often removed to free up the space needed. Most patients didn't survive these efforts.

Throughout the years, Waverly Hills provided health care for thousands of patients. With the amount of people being admitted to the hospital, you can imagine the amount of deaths as well. Records show that over 60,000 patients died while at Waverly Hills. Eventually, the amount of TB cases diminished as a cure was found. Tuberculosis sanatoriums were no longer needed for their specialized treatments. So Waverly Hills closed its doors in the early 1960s.

In 1962, the building reopened as a sanitarium for elderly people. The name was changed to Woodhaven Geriatrics

Sanitarium. The conditions remained the same and, as some people would say, they got much worse. More experiments were conducted on patients during this era until eventually, in the 1970s, the building was closed down again. It has remained closed ever since.

There are some stories that although the hospital was closed, it didn't keep people out. One of the tales is of a cult that practiced their sacrificial ceremonies in the building. Rumor has it a homeless man and his dog, seeking refuge there, became one of the sacrifices. These may just be tall tales, but they were stories that I heard during my visit to Waverly Hills.

If any place in the United States could be haunted, it would have to be this one. With all the highly emotional occurrences that ran rampant in these rooms, it sure does lend potential for spirits to roam the empty halls. If tragedy, pain, suffering, death and sadness can cause a location to hold onto and replay its

Look at the pale ghost ..wait that's me

past, then Waverly Hills is like a sponge, a sponge that is holding onto these forms of energy, and every once in awhile, releases some for us to view. There is so much to explore here and each experience brings new ghostly tales for us to share.

Conference

My friend Matt and I were set to head down to Louisville after work on Friday. Len and Kim were going to meet us at the hotel that night. In fact, due to Matt's mad driving skills, we passed Len and Kim on the way. I remember it very well, because a few days before, I met Linda Blair. When I met Linda, I had her sign a photo for Len so he could have a memento of my visit to her. When we passed Len, I made sure to hold the signed photo up in the window so he'd see it. Call it a tease if you want, but it almost made him wreck his car since he has a bit of a "thing" for Ms. Blair.

We ended up getting to Louisville around 8 p.m. and by this point, we were famished. Matt, Len, Kim and I all met up for food and conversation. If you ever sit down with the four of us, you never know where the conversation is going to end up. This was one of those nights as were laughing hysterically at every little thing. I am sure we were quite a disturbance for those around us, but we were in our own little world so we didn't care. After dinner we headed back to the hotel so we could get some sleep before heading out to Waverly Hills the following morning.

Matt and I woke up (in separate beds mind you) around 6 a.m. We probably didn't get to bed the night before until around midnight. So at this point, six hours of sleep was going to have to suffice. We went down to our complimentary continental breakfast that consisted of stale cereal and doughnuts. Then we hooked up with the Adams posse and headed out to Waverly.

One of the greatest things about Waverly is the drive up to the site. You literally are going through a nice little neighborhood of sweet little homes. Then you turn past a golf course and start heading up this hill. Woods grace both sides of the graveled road, which seems to really set a gloomy mood. Once you reach the top of the hill, it opens up into this huge area of land that was once a bustling hospital. I can only compare this view to the panoramic shot of the Stanley Hotel in the movie *The Shining*. The building was massive and it was going to be our playground. Oh yes, it was going to be our playground.

After parking, we started to explore a bit but were eventually ushered into the former laundry building of the hospital. This was to be where most of the conference activities were going to be held. Getting into the hospital was going to have to wait until dark. Although I wanted nothing more than to enter the building, I was a bit afraid of the LGHS security. I decided I'd wait to go into the hospital, rather than try to get in and need a hospital myself. There was going to be enough stuff to keep me occupied so it was no big deal to me.

Inside the outer building, all the speakers were setting up their tables. There were a lot of other things going on here as well. Exhibits and vendors included authors, tattoo artists, tarot

Here's a view of the back of the building

card readers and jewelry designers, to name a few. There was even a camera that would take a photo of your aura. That was pretty interesting and although I didn't do it, I was intrigued by those who did. I did, however, do the tarot card reading. The girl who did was very good. She was able to nail a lot about me and issues that I was dealing with at the time. At this point the weekend was looking good for me!

We were able to get a tour of the grounds with one of the LGHS members eventually. It was very informative and I felt that I learned quite a bit about how everything operated back in its day. I took a lot of photos during this time but found it very difficult because of the hospital's massive size. For every minute that passed, we were itching to get inside that much more. Unfortunately, we were quite a ways off from that time, so we just had to keep ourselves busy. After the tour we went and got some lunch and then came back to the hospital.

After listening to some speakers and wandering around a bit more, time began to fly by. The table directly across from Troy had a trailer for another film about the Bell Witch looping. I think I had every word of that trailer memorized by the end of the day. Even though I saw it 40-plus times, there's a part with a girl screaming that always seemed to make me jump. To kill some more time I checked out the schedule and realized that the dinner break was rapidly approaching. I was really looking forward to dinner as I was getting very hungry. It was going to be a nice barbeque meal with all the fixings. Although I had that bad experience at the Bell Witch Festival, I had faith Keith Age and his team could pull this one off. Around 7 p.m. we all marched over to an area near the "death tunnel" for our meal. I thought it was kind of funny to be sitting there. Imagine yourself going to a restaurant and the host would say, "Smoking, Non-Smoking or Death Tunnel?"

Dinner was perfect! Although we did have one interesting event happen during our meal. To this day, I shiver when I think about it. If you are at home reading this, please make sure all the lights are on. If you are alone you may want to put the book down and watch reruns of "Roseanne" or something. For those of you still reading, here we go.

Sitting at our table were the following people. Hopefully I remember everyone, but I am sure I'll forget a couple. Troy

Taylor was sitting at the head of the table. On one side it was me, my friend Matt and Roberta Simpson Brown (great storyteller!) On the other side of the table it was Len, Kim and Bill Alsing. We were all partaking in the food that lay before us when this strange young man walked up to the table. He walked straight to Troy and just stood there staring for what seemed like forever. Then "it" spoke. I will try to do this to the best of my ability. Hopefully I can recreate the conversation so you can truly experience what we did. It was an amazing thing to witness.

    Troy said: "Can I help you?"
    It said: "Are you Troy Taylor?"
    Troy said: "Yes I am."
    It said: "You were in that movie *St. Francisville Experiment*, right?"
    Troy said: "Yes, and I can't give you your money back." Everyone at the table laughed at that comment and then proceeded to continue not making eye contact.
    It said: "No, I loved it!"
    Troy said: "Ummm, Okay."
    It said: "Can I ask you something?"
    Troy said: "Sure."
    It said: "In that one part of the movie, where the girl is looking in the mirror and she gets attacked. Is she okay?"
    Troy said: "Yeah, she's fine. It was just a movie."
    It said: "Okay, good. I was worried that she may have gotten hurt badly from that."
    Troy said, "Nope she made it through okay."

    It was at this point there was just a very awkward silence as the kid still stood looking at us.
    I tried my hardest not to make eye contact, but found it difficult as there was something very odd about him. The whole time the kid stood there, he just seemed really different. His wardrobe consisted of black pants with a black dress shirt and a purple vest. After a few minutes of us taking little nibbles of our food as to not get finished eating while he stood there, he walked away. Roberta, who is an absolute sweetheart, observed: "Something is wrong with that boy."
    The kid then got his food and sat at another table in a

position where he would be looking directly at Troy while he ate. This was even creepier as the kid's eyes would peer over his hamburger as he took a bite. The stare was always fixed unblinkingly on Troy. The rest of the night Len, Matt and I were on security duty for Troy. Any time we saw the kid get near, we would circle Troy and escort him away. The whole thing may have been an exaggeration on our part, but we did feel very strange around this kid. Fortunately, we didn't see him too many times the rest of the night.

Dinner probably was over at around 8:30 p.m. Everyone was being divided into groups for the exploration of Waverly. We thought that we would immediately go into the building to start our investigations but that was not the case. Everyone was just kind of standing around waiting for the door to open. Len, Matt and I were very slaphappy at this point since we had been up for 14 hours and we knew we'd be up for about eight more. This is where the real show started. It was now time for the stooges to entertain.

We started out kind of slow, just chatting to a few people. Eventually we were standing up as other people were sitting down listening to our antics. By the time an hour passed, we had quite the group around us. I am not real sure what we all did. I do know that it involved some jokes, a lot of bad puns, some dancing and I believe we may have sung a few songs. Either way, we kept the crowd entertained, which was a good thing since we didn't actually enter the building until about 11 p.m.

Finally, our dreams had come true! We were about to embark on an overnight investigation of the famous, very haunted Waverly Hills Sanatorium. Well, at least we thought that was the case. We were all corralled into the former cafeteria. There we had to listen to another speaker. Nothing against the speaker or anything, but I was ready to investigate, not to listen to a presentation again. At this point, I had been up for 17 hours straight. Now, the floor of Waverly Hills is full of debris including dust, rust, plaster flakes, etc. I was surprised at how very comfortable it was when I lay down to take a nap on it. Of course I didn't fall asleep. I didn't want to have the presentation finish, everyone leave, and wake up all alone.

About 12:30, the presentation was over and now we were going to investigate the sanatorium. We were all put back into our groups and each was given a location to investigate. Just when we got into Waverly, we were escorted out as our first stop was the front of the building OUTSIDE! It was very entertaining as once we got outside, it was almost like the investigation had a shotgun start. We were all looking at the building when all of a sudden, every window seemed to light up with camera flashes. It was almost like everyone was ready to take a picture as soon as the gun sounded the start of the investigation.

Walking around the outside of the building was all right. Nothing really exciting happened. The grounds were set up with a cemetery theme for the haunted house promotion they were doing at the time. Although it wasn't a real cemetery, it did help set the mood. I know I shouldn't try to scare people on investigations, but sometimes opportunities arise that you can't pass up. I ended up hiding behind one of the tombstones waiting for someone to walk past. It was probably about 15 minutes before someone did. By this time my knees started aching and feeling very sore and tired. So by the time I jumped up for my big entrance, it was more of a mediocre attempt than a surprise attack. The outcome was just a little jump by the unsuspecting victim. What a waste of time that was.

Eventually, our time outside ran its course and it was time to head back inside. This proved to be unfortunate for Len's wife, Kim. As we walked down the sidewalk, Kim stepped off the side of it and tumbled down. In doing this, she really injured her ankle and couldn't go any farther on the investigation. She ended up returning to the hotel to ice her foot. We started with 15 people in our group, now we were down to 14.

Once we got inside, we began to explore all the different areas of the building. We'd spend some time on the first floor for a bit. Then we'd move up to all the different floors and areas throughout the night. Since I don't remember what order we went to each location, the logical thing would be for me to just talk about each place starting with the first floor. Won't you come with me on this written, guided tour?

For the most part, the floors were very similar. The lower floors contained a lot of the medical facilities. One of my favorite rooms from this area was the one where they would drain the bodies of fluids after the patients had passed away. It was a very creepy room, as every patient who died in the hospital would have come through there. You can still see the drains where the fluids would go and it seemed to be a lot colder around that area. It could have just been our imagination, but several people acknowledged the temperature change.

To me, the most exciting part of the night was going on the third and fourth floors. I need to use this time to try and describe how this hospital was set up. Please use the photo for reference. There was a large hallway that ran the length of the back of the building. On one side of the hallway were large windows and on the other side were patient rooms. The hallway could be looked at in three sections. If you start from one end of the building, there'd be an atrium room. Then you'd walk down the hallway for a bit and it would angle to the left. That's where a nurse's station was located. Then you'd proceed down a hallway again and it would eventually angle to the left again. Another nurse's station would be there. Finally, the hallway would run into another atrium-type room. So when standing outside and looking at the building it was like a half circle only it had more of an angle to it instead of a curve. I really hope that makes sense. Especially since I've kind of confused myself trying to explain how the hospital was set up.

The patient rooms on the side of this hallway had two entrances to them. One entrance led to the large hallway with the windows. The other entrance led to a smaller hallway. So imagine yourself standing in the large hallway with the windows. Your back would be against these windows. Now, take a step into one of the patient rooms. Take a look around, sit down if you'd like and then proceed through the other door in the room. This would bring us deeper into the building. Now you are standing in a smaller hallway. The patient room you were just in is directly behind you. Straight ahead of you is another room. These rooms are much smaller then the previous ones. Okay, I'm getting confused again, but please hang in there. This explanation does have a purpose.

This is how the second, third and fourth floors were set up. The rooms in the center of the two hallways were used for patients who still had a fighting chance to defeat TB. They were in these rooms so they could have their beds wheeled out into the hallway for some of that Kentucky fresh air. As I stated before, fresh air was one of the only known treatments for TB.

All the windows along that hall never had glass; they had screens so the fresh air could circulate. The rooms on the other side of the smaller hallway were used for patients who were already too far into the disease and were not expected to make it. Rumor has it that some rich people were able to stay in much nicer rooms no matter how ill they were.

Now that you know the building's layout, I can officially get into the coolest paranormal activity I have ever seen. If you stand in the center of the smaller hallway on the third or fourth floors, you can actually see shadow people moving about. The trick to doing this is to rely heavily on your peripheral vision. While standing still, you'll look down the hallway and fix your eyes on the nurse's station. This is where the building angles, so it gives you something to stare at instead of just staring down an endless hallway. Moonlight will actually shine through the windows of the large hallway. The light will then filter through both doorways of the middle rooms and will then illuminate the little hallway where you stand. It's not a lot of light, but it's enough.

As you stare down the hallway, you will sometimes see shadows moving around. Sometimes it's just for a second and sometimes it's much longer. We watched one shadow walk down the hall right towards us. It got real tense because we weren't sure what to do. We didn't know if we should run, or just stand there. As it got closer, it ended up just dissipating in front of us. This was much to the delight of those who could see it. As it turns out, usually about 60 to 70 percent of the spectators could actually see the shadows. At one point, when the shadows were moving around, we could hear the sound of metal clanking together. We couldn't figure out what the sound was. I walked down the hall where we had been seeing the shadows to see if I could figure it out. As I stood there listening, I leaned back against the wall. When I did this, my ring hit a metal handrail that ran the length of the hallway. It made the same exact sound that we heard before. Was the noise we heard a patient walking down the hallway holding onto the handrail for support? Who knows? But we do know what we saw on those two floors and we have no explanation for it.

There was a little more excitement on the fifth floor of the building. We were down to about six or eight people in our group by our time. This floor was where some of the worse-off patients were. Some of them were suffering from mental issues. Two nurses actually committed suicide inside one of the rooms. One hanged herself and the other jumped out the window. Some people believe that they may have been murdered and the murderer covered it up as if it were a suicide. That's a whole different story that I won't go into.

I remember going up to the fifth floor and wandering around. About fifteen minutes later, Matt and I realized that Len had disappeared. Again this is a no-no on paranormal investigations. Matt and I walked away from the rest of the group to find Len. We expected to see him laying on the floor crying in the fetal position, but we weren't that lucky. We did, however, find him frozen in terror in room 502. This was the room where the nurses died. Len didn't know that at the time, but he felt drawn to that room. When he got in there, he said he just couldn't move at all. He felt as if something was holding him in place. A theory that Len and I have is that Len may have possibly walked into a re-enactment of the hanging that took place. When you have a residual haunting, where an event plays itself over and over again, is it possible to become part of that event? We think you can. We think that if you interfere with that situation, you may feel the emotion or the pain that the person felt during that time. So when Len was frozen in fear, was he frozen to represent the lifeless body of the nurse hanging in the room? We may never know, but we will monitor this theory as we continue to investigate.

Once we left the fifth floor, we were heading to our last stop of the night. This stop was actually the one I was most looking forward to. Lo and behold, we were off to see the death tunnel! By the time we approached the tunnel entrance, we were down to six people in our group. The death tunnel was an actual tunnel that ran from the hospital, down a steep hill about 480 feet. The tunnel was used for several purposes, however the most intriguing was for transporting bodies from the hospital. When patients died and were drained of their fluids, they were removed from the building via the tunnel. This was done so that the surviving patients wouldn't see how many bodies were leaving every day. The staff felt if patients saw this, they would lose hope and give up their fight against TB.

This is the entrance to the Death Tunnel

Although the patients were already dead when they were taken down the tunnel, it is still a place of interest for ghost hunters. Out of our six remaining group members, only four of us walked down the tunnel. The walk was very difficult since the steps aren't consistent. You'd have a few short steps, and then a platform, then some more steps, and another platform. With this layout, it was very difficult to build momentum so it seemed to tire you out quicker. Once we reached the bottom, we realized that now we had to climb back up. I am not going to sugar coat this, it sucked! It was about 4:30 a.m. We had been up for 22 ½ hours at this point. We did make it to the top and at that point we were ready to leave.

Matt and I said our goodbyes and began our four-hour drive home. Matt started getting tired about half way back, so I took over the driving duties. For the first time in my driving career, I think I fell asleep at the wheel. I'm not sure if I did or not, but I remember the terrain looking different when I opened my eyes. Not to mention the rear of the car that I was quickly approaching. I hit the brakes and swerved into the other lane, which woke Matt up. He then made the decision of pulling over at a rest stop and we took a nap in the car. A couple of hours later we woke up and made it home alive.

Yet Another Waverly Overnight!

A couple of years ago, I had another opportunity to go to Waverly Hills. This time I went with Troy Taylor's American Hauntings Tours. Matt was supposed to go with us, but the morning we were leaving he got sick and had to go home. Although I felt bad that Matt couldn't join us, it didn't matter because Waverly is like Disney World to me.

We arrived early in the afternoon before Troy and company showed up. We walked around the hotel a bit. The hotel has its share of ghosts as well. Within an hour of being there, we had our first bit of excitement. I won't go into too much detail, but we saw a man run a motorcycle into the back of a van at a stoplight. As the guy fell off the bike, he got up, looked at it, and started running down the street. I got a kick out of it because he was holding his pants up while he ran. Turned out the bike was stolen. Most of us who were standing there looked at each other in amazement like, "did that just happen?" I wasn't sure how the trip would top that, but I knew it would somehow.

This trip was actually more centered on haunted Louisville then just Waverly Hills. We stayed in a haunted hotel, we went to a haunted theater, we took a tour with Mr. Ghostwalker, and at the end of the night we all went to Waverly Hills. Although I would have rather spent more time at Waverly, seeing these other places that I didn't get a chance to before was a great experience as well.

At the end of the night we made our way to Waverly Hills. They were having their own tours going on that night and the place was hoppin.' The money from these kinds of tours is what is helping to pay for renovations to the historic building. You can actually see the improvement every time you go there. We waited around until most of the other tours left before we went in for a look-see.

I think the amount of people and energy that were there that night really stirred things up! There were a lot of sightings of shadow people again that night. At one point we turned down a hall on the fourth floor and we saw something moving around. It turned out to be a bat and it scared the heck out of all of us. On the third floor, we saw a shadow person right away. One of the LGHS members shined his laser pointer at the shadow and the light actually stopped on the edge of the shadow. It didn't go through the shadow and hit the wall. This showed that the shadow may have had mass! Another interesting thing from this floor was when I looked down the hall, I could see blocks of light. This was created by light shining through the doorways of the center rooms. So it would appear in the hallway as a block of light, then dark, then light, then dark and so on. While watching this area, you could see a shadow pass across a block of light. The only way to re-create this was for a person to stand in that room and walk from one side to the other. It was very interesting.

Down one of the halls towards the end of the building, we actually saw a red glow hover above the floor. The story in this area is there was a woman who happened to be quite the smoker. Often times, if you leave a cigarette in the vicinity of that room, it will disappear when you return. Along with the disappearing cigarettes, the smell of smoke will waft through the room. Or in our case, the faint red glow of a lit cigarette will weave in and out of the rooms at that end of the building. What we saw could possibly have been related to this phenomenon.

During this event, we were actually just doing more of a walkthrough and not a full-fledged investigation. When we got to the death tunnel, since I didn't learn my lesson the first time, I walked down it again. Once down there, I realized I forgot I had to climb back up the stairs again. As painful as it was, I would have kicked myself if I didn't go down it, so I'm glad I did.

We all headed back to the hotel around midnight and set off for home the next morning. It was a jam-packed couple of days and I would recommend it to anyone and everyone! Louisville is a great town with a lot of history and to not go would be doing yourself a disservice.

Lessons Learned:

1. Never wander off alone - for several reasons. First, you could get hurt. Second, you don't have a witness for documenting occurrences. Third, just for safety reasons.

2. Be mindful of what Len eats when spending an entire day with him.

XI. LINCOLN THEATER - DECATUR, ILLINOIS

The Lincoln Theater was built in 1916 on the site of the former Arcade Hotel. The Arcade Hotel was destroyed by a terrible fire in 1915. Records show that several people died in that fire. But as the saying goes, "every new beginning comes from some other beginning's end." It's because of the fire that we have this great vaudeville theater today. Several famous people performed there including Bob Hope and Harry Houdini.

I have had the opportunity to investigate the theater on several occasions. The first time was several years ago when they did an overnight investigation around Halloween. This was a blast and although we personally didn't have anything happen, I heard a lot of people did. Most common were footsteps on the stage. Even though we weren't fortunate enough to be followed by the footsteps, we were one of the few who stayed all night! Now that I think about it, that wasn't really all that cool since we were exhausted the entire next day.

A couple of years back, Troy returned to Decatur to get back to the days of old with his tours and special events. Yes folks, finally, Troy Taylor has returned to Decatur, Illinois! Len and I were excited about it because finally we would be able to take over Alton and it also gave us an insider to some great haunted locations in Decatur. One of those locations was the historic Lincoln Theater.

In February of 2007, Troy hosted the annual "Dead of Winter" event (then titled Weird Winter) at the Lincoln Theater. A day full of speakers who helped contribute to the "Weird" book series was just the beginning. During the presentations a lot of people reported seeing shadows on the mezzanine level and some reported the sensation of a person sitting behind them even though the seats were empty. Some people even felt someone tap them on the shoulder while they sat in the auditorium. All these things were great, but the good stuff was yet to come. Once the conference was over, it was time for the overnight investigation of the theater.

During the investigation, we divided everybody up into four groups of about ten to twelve people. Each group would spend thirty minutes in four different areas. The first location was the basement, which included dressing rooms and a utility room. Then there was the stage area, which included, well, the stage and also a very cool spiral staircase that led up to the catwalk. The third location was the auditorium and lastly there was the mezzanine/balcony combo. After thirty minutes each group would meet in the lobby and then they'd be directed to a new location. Once all four groups had investigated each area they would be free to roam the building.

I was in charge of the basement, so it didn't matter what group it was, if they were heading to the basement, I was their guy. I am grateful for this because I experienced something very interesting in the basement that night.

I brought the group down into the basement and told them a bit of the history of the place. Houdini performed there and the trapdoor he had the theater owners cut into the floor was still there to this day. Of course everyone wanted to see it. Now I must tell you, I hadn't been to the theater for several years. There had been a lot of renovations done since the last time I was there. I searched and searched for about ten minutes but couldn't seem to find the door. After seeing the sad faces of the group I decided to go up on the stage (directly above the basement) and see if Len could find it. I left everyone in the capable hands of "Crazy" Steve.

When I got up to the stage, Len was looking pretty worn out from escorting people up the spiral staircase. I suggested he look for the door and I'd take the rest up the stairs. Len was pleased and he headed down to the basement. I finished taking the people up to the catwalk and then we just stood around center stage. The lights were out, making it very dark, especially with the stage curtain closed. After standing still for about five minutes, all ten of us heard someone run across the stage behind us. I shined my flashlight toward the back of the stage and didn't see anyone there. Then I took a couple of victims, I mean volunteers, with me to look behind the curtain. That area was used for storage, so unless the person I heard running could have jumped over a baby grand piano and maneuvered around some track lighting, there was no way anyone could have been there. My next thought was maybe someone was running in the basement and the sound carried up to the stage. A few minutes later Len came hobbling back to the stage. I asked if he had someone get scared and run through the basement. He was positive that nobody was running downstairs. So we may have actually had an encounter within the first 30 minutes of investigating. It didn't end there either.

Time was up and we needed to get everybody back to the lobby. I opened the door to a small hallway for people to leave the stage. If they turned right, it would have taken them down to the basement. I made sure everyone turned left, walked down a small hallway, and then through a door leading into the auditorium. From there they would be able to reach the lobby. Len was the last to walk through the door and I told him I was going to go downstairs and get my group. This was where the night got a little hairy.

When I got to the basement, I walked through the hallway where the dressing rooms were and followed it back to the far depths of the dark basement. When I got all the way into the back of basement, I realized that I was quite possibly alone. I didn't see anyone around and I assumed that Steve took them all up to the lobby. Since I wasn't sure of that, I decided to check each of the dressing rooms. I opened the first door and nearly wet myself. Turns out that the first thing you see when opening that door is your reflection in one of the mirrors. After regaining my composure, I closed the door and started to move on. Well, I would have moved on if I didn't hear a voice behind me say "hello." I spun around and whipped out my flashlight like a six-shooter. I looked behind me and didn't see anyone. I thought maybe Steve was still down there so I walked to where his camera had been set up, but it was gone. At this point I was a little concerned, but I blew it off to being just my imagination.

I proceeded down the hall and checked the rest of the dressing rooms. I was able to confirm everyone was gone. When I reached for the door that leads to the stairs, I heard an all too familiar voice again. "HELLO," it said, much louder this time. Actually, the voice was either louder or closer to me, I'm not sure which. I spun around again, this time holding the flashlight more like a shotgun. Yet again, there was no one there. This time the hair on my neck stood up. I got goose bumps everywhere and I hightailed it upstairs.

As I walked through the short hallway that leads to the auditorium my heart was pounding. As if what happened in the basement wasn't enough, I pushed the door to the auditorium and it wouldn't open. This was not looking good for me. I pushed it several times and each time it would give just a little and then it would slam back at me. Finally, I put everything I had into the door and it opened. That's when I heard John Winterbauer laughing. It turned out that Len told John I was getting my group from the basement and John thought it would be funny to hold the door shut on me. It takes a lot to get me mad, and I give four marks to John for getting me to that level. Had it been any other time, I would have laughed along with him. In this case, his timing was awful since I was already freaking out.

John then looked behind me and asked, "Where's your group?"

I said, "They must be in the lobby with Steve." John looked surprised.

He asked, "Who were you talking to before you tried to open the door?"

I said, "Why do you ask?"

John then said, "I was standing on the other side of this door for a couple of minutes. I know I heard a conversation on the other side of the door."

I told him that I hadn't been talking to anybody, although somebody had been trying to talk to me. Here John and I both experienced something very peculiar and we were only about 50 feet from each other at the time. Yet, we didn't hear the same thing. Although I was still reeling from being totally freaked out, we were also both very excited to share our story with everyone.

In June of 2007 we were back at the theater again. This time it was for the American Ghost Society Conference. Len and I were very fortunate to host a segment called "Sons of Strange Stuff." While Len and I were speaking I saw a shadow person in one of the far right mezzanine seats. I didn't say anything but was able to see if for a few seconds and then it simply vanished.

That night, we had another investigation of the theater. It was set up identically to the way we did it at the Weird Winter event. I took each group to the basement, shared my previous experience with them and then sent them off to investigate. This evening was a lot quieter then the previous time, although we did have one thing happen in the basement. One of my patrons opened the utility room door and instantly screamed and backed away from the slamming door. I saw her reaction and it was very genuine. She said she saw a man standing in the room looking right at her. It was very quick and only a glimpse but that was what she saw. Although her reaction showed how scared she was, it doesn't mean that what she saw was a ghost. It could have been her imagination. Whether it was a ghost or a trick of the mind, her reaction would have been the same because they both would catch a person off guard.

Even though the weekend investigations were a bit slower, the theater seems to always catch us off guard with its many spirits. It's when you least expect something to happen that the theater displays its charm to you. If you ever get a chance to visit this theater, please do! And by all means, if you have any spare change, donate it to the renovation of this great building. I guarantee you the money is going to the right thing because I have seen the improvements over the years.

Lessons Learned

1. Always try to find people who experienced the same thing. Having multiple witnesses adds to the validity of an event.

2. Know where John Winterbauer is at all times.

XII. HAUNTED ALTON - A THREE-HOUR TOUR

A few years back Troy asked me if I'd be interested in being a tour guide for the Haunted Alton Ghost Tours. I had been on these tours so many times that I already knew the stories, so it was a no-brainer for me to accept the offer! I always enjoyed the tours and to actually be the guy telling the stories was thrilling to me. Not to mention the fact that I enjoy the spotlight every once in awhile. Of course, that's only when Len lets me in the spotlight.

What I'd like to do in this chapter is give you a shortened, trimmed-down guided tour of Alton. Please do not let this keep you from actually taking one of our tours. They are so much better in person standing in or around the actual locations. I am also not including every one of our stops in this section. I am focusing on areas that I have experienced strange activity through my tours or through investigations.

Although we never guarantee anything to happen, stuff often does. If something does happen, it's never something that we made happen. We do not use parlor tricks to try and scare our people. The stories sell themselves and that's all you need. I'd appreciate if during this part of the tour you would turn off your cell phones so this chapter is uninterrupted. You'll thank me later as you are hanging on every word, unable to put the book down, only to have your cell phone ring and it either scares you to death, or kills the mood entirely. Other than that simple rule, enjoy your private tour. It's just you, me and some great history and stories.

Before I get started, I do have to say that my favorite part of our tours is the history. Anyone can lead somebody to an area that's had activity, and tell them it's haunted. But it adds so much more to a story to be taken somewhere and told why it's haunted. When history and actual fact help explain what happened, it really adds a personal touch to the story. That's how our tours are. We don't use any psychic abilities or other methods to explain what's happening. We use years of research through historical records to explain everything. It's what we do and the 1,000+ yearly tour patrons appreciate that.

Here I am telling stories to a tour group. By the time I am finished, I usually pass out from exhaustion) Photo by Charles Carron

HISTORY AND HAUNTINGS BOOK COMPANY

This is the base of operations for our tour. It's a great place to begin the tours because of the atmosphere. We are literally surrounded by books on history and ghosts. Does it get any better than that? Arriving early for the tour is a good move as you get better parking, and you can kill time by browsing through the huge selection of books.

For those of you who have been there before, there's a creepy little ghost guy that stands in the corner. It's one of those dolls that stand about three feet tall and look like a child. A lot of times you'll see these at homes standing against the wall as if counting for a game of hide and seek. That's the kind of thing this is, only this one is wearing a ghost costume. I don't know what it is about the thing, but it just creeps me out. Every once in awhile, I find myself looking under the sheet just to make sure it's fake.

When our tours are completed, we always end up back at the bookstore. Often, people like to come in, do some shopping and listen to more stories. We love when this happens as sometimes it's hard for us to quit talking. There have been nights where we would get back to the store around 10:30 and I wouldn't leave until 1a.m. because people want to keep hearing stories. Although I don't mind this

Here's the little bugger staring at me with those big beady eyes

one bit, it means it's later at night once the customers leave and I am all alone. I then have to walk around the store and shut off all the lights. This part is very eerie. I know one of these times when I am shutting off the lights, I am going to see that little ghost kid take off running behind a bookshelf. Believe me when I say, if that happens, I will probably start crying. That would just freak me out beyond belief.

On one occasion upon returning with the tour, that ghost kid was turned in a different direction. My initial reaction was someone moved it. A woman mentioned that she was standing by that area the entire time I was initially speaking at the store, and the ghost was never moved. I began to laugh about it and say that someone had to have moved it. Once everyone was out of the store I began shutting off the lights. Much to my surprise, the ghost kid was back where he should have been. Since I was busy telling stories, I never noticed if someone moved it. It's very possible someone was playing a trick on me, but I guess I'll never know.

We do have a feeling that the store is haunted. Back when it first opened it was a bakery, this we know for sure. We have also heard that the owner's son died when he was nine years old. I am sure that little boy is haunting the store. Several times we have had things disappear and reappear days later. Books have fallen off the shelves, books will change positions on the shelves over night, and footsteps will walk across the floor. We've even had the front door open and close with nobody in sight. The spirit there is definitely not threatening to us; it's merely playful.

We like to start the tour off with some rules for participants to follow. After that we go into some brief Alton history. We feel that Alton got its start back in 1814. A man named Colonel Rufus Easton operated a ferry service upriver. Easton made a fortune from this business venture because a lot of people were heading out west and needed to cross the river. Although today we think of St. Louis as the gateway to the west, most people don't realize that many settlers filtered down to St. Louis by going through Alton first. It was at this time that Colonel Easton decided that the bluffs along the river would be a great place for a city.

Easton began selling plots of land in an area he named Alton, after his eldest son. Streets like Alby, Langdon and Henry were named after some of his other children. Buyers were eating this property up and yet again Easton was becoming wealthy on another business venture. But by 1819 a group of land speculators came into the area and found that Easton didn't own any of the land that he was selling. The legal battles were tied up in court for years and became very expensive for Easton.

In 1821, Easton ended up in St. Louis, Missouri, where he became state attorney general. He was the Post Master of St. Charles, Mo., where his daughter Mary helped found Lindenwood College. Her spirit is said to haunt the campus. Col. Easton died in 1834.

ENOS SANATORIUM

This massive structure was built in 1857 by Nathanial Hanson. It was an enormous mansion that stood high above all the other homes in the area. While most people would think that Hanson was building this impressive structure to show off his wealth, there was actually a more personal reason. This home was designed and built to help runaway slaves traverse the Underground Railroad.

Although above ground the building was a beautiful Victorian home, it was the basement that truly made this place special. Under the front yard was a specially designed tunnel resting about 15 feet below the street that runs in front of the home. I use the term tunnel loosely as it was actually a long room. It had the appearance of a tunnel because of the narrow width and arched ceiling. It didn't lead to other places around Alton as the term "tunnel" may lead you to believe. I'm not sure how many slaves would have been kept in this room, nor am I sure how long they would have stayed there. I'd have to assume the answers would be as many as could fit and how ever long it took.

During this time, anyone caught aiding slaves on their way to freedom would often be lynched in their own front yard. They'd be beaten, hanged, whatever was necessary to get the message across to people that this was an unacceptable practice. Back then, slaves were considered nothing more than expensive farm equipment. They weren't human; they were

The Lighter Side of Darkness -- Page 111

property. If you were caught with another man's property, then you were stealing. This was considered the "law" back then and many people were abused and murdered because of their humanitarian impulse to aid the slaves.

In order to not be discovered, the Hanson family had to design some kind of system to let the slaves know when it was safe to come to the house. Atop the building was a large cupola that appeared to be more of a watchtower. If it was safe to approach, the Hanson family would place a single lantern in the cupola window. If there was danger, two lanterns would be placed in the window. As the slaves would approach the river, they'd look up at the cupola and know instantly if they should advance or stay put. If there was indeed a single light in the window, they'd make their way across the river and into the carriage house next to the Hanson home. They would then be escorted into a tunnel that led to the sub-basement holding area. There they would stay until it was safe to move on to the next stop on the all-important road to freedom. The Hanson family made it through the slavery years without ever being caught. The building stayed in the family's possession for many years. Around 1911, the building finally changed hands and a Dr. W.H. Enos was the new owner.

Enos used this building as a tuberculosis sanatorium during his tenure in Alton. It seemed to be more of a rest home, as there was no cure for TB at that time. Patients would spend most of their time next to the open windows. The patients would also spend a lot of their time eating good, rich, wholesome food. These were the only things that could be done to fight the disease. Enos ended up losing around a hundred patients each of his first three years. He wasn't going to be put off by the staggering death toll. He decided to remedy the situation by literally "raising the roof" on the old building.

In 1914, Dr. Enos had the roof lifted up and a a third story added. This enabled him to care for more patients. He also attached a building to the side of the sanatorium. This building was going to be used for around-the-clock health care. Nurses and doctors would live in these quarters so they would be available at all hours. But the extra floor only increased the number of patients who lost their lives in this building. Enos sold the building after about ten years. Since then, it has housed apartments.

This is the point where the ghost stories began to develop. Tenants who rented rooms in the former sanatorium have experienced a steady flow of paranormal occurrences, from having doors open and close, lights turn on and off, disembodied voices, etc. It seemed that most often things would happen when renovations were being done. Perhaps it's the spirits' desire to keep their home unchanged that stirs them up. It could also be that changing something about an old building releases a spirit into our realm. We may never know, but the whole idea of renovations causing activity is something that may definitely have some merit.

We are not sure who or what is haunting this place. Could it be the slaves that traveled through here on their way to safety? We are very fortunate to know that this building was part of the Underground Railroad, since no records were kept by participants due to the fact that involvement was against the law. Going along with the lack of Underground Railroad information, we do not know for sure if any slaves died here. I'm not saying that you need a death for a place to be haunted, but in a lot of cases, that is usually the cause. I am sure that this building still houses a lot of the emotions felt by the runaway slaves who were housed here. Whether it's hunger, fear, sickness, sadness or pain, this energy and emotion was soaked up into the stone that lines the tunnel's walls. This energy will sometimes retell the struggles that these slaves endured during their voyage to safety. The walls will speak, if only we would take the time to listen.

I think a greater cause of this building being haunted is due to the number of patients who died here during its tenure as a TB hospital. These patients suffered terribly and I'm sure they left their emotional energy in the building as well. Since the former hospital rooms are now apartments, it seems to be logical that the patients are causing the upstairs activity. I do feel that some of the lower building activity is caused by the spirits of escaped slaves.

Two stories I like to tell on the tour involve tenants who lived in the building for just a short period of time. Like the couple who were celebrating one evening with a nice dinner. The husband had brought home an expensive bottle of wine to top the dinner off. He placed the bottle on the dining room table and headed to the kitchen to help his wife finish preparing dinner. As they began bringing the food to the table, they both noticed the bottle of wine was gone. The door was still locked, the windows were closed and they were the only "living" souls in the apartment. Not to be put off by this, they sat down and had a lovely meal together. A few days later, the missing bottle of wine reappeared on the back of the toilet tank in the bathroom. It seems to me that this would have been noticed very quickly if it had been mistakenly placed there by the man when he brought it home. That wasn't the case, as they swore up and down it wasn't there when they frequented the bathroom. They did, however, drink the wine and said it tasted great. Perhaps that extra three days it was gone made it age a little more so the taste was improved.

Another story I really like involved a woman who was staying in one of the second floor apartments. She told us how late at night, it would sound as if someone was moving around in the apartment above her. One night, she had gone out with a friend and when they returned, the noise was happening again. She said it sounded as if someone upstairs was moving an old couch, the kind with the big round feet. The noise sounded like someone was picking up the couch on one end, dragging it across the floor and dropping it. Then they would move to the other end of the couch, pick it up again and drag it in the other direction. This happened several times until it finally pushed her to the boiling point. She marched up the stairs and began to knock on the door. At that point, the noise inside the apartment was so loud that she made a fist and began pounding on the door. Just then, the door slowly opened revealing not only no tenants, but also no furniture! The woman raced back down to her apartment, locked the door and spent the rest of the evening scared to death. The next morning she contacted the landlord and found out no one had lived in that apartment for weeks.

As of 2006, we have been able to take our tours into the tunnel underneath this building. This has been a treat because we are actually going into an area of great historical importance. It's also a spot where we have had strange things happen on our tours. Normally we have a lot of participants and in order to go into the basement, we need to divide the group in half. When I get people down to that tunnel, I like to turn out all the lights. I try setting the mood the same way the slaves would have had it when they were hiding. Interestingly, I have found that when I prod people into the tunnel, most people will immediately walk in and put their backs to the wall. Very seldom will someone stand in the middle of the tunnel. I think this is a defense mechanism where we feel safer when we don't think our backs are vulnerable. It's because of people lining the walls that we are sometimes able to experience the sound of someone walking down the center of the tunnel. Very faintly you will hear the sound of shuffling feet in the dirt and dust. Sometimes our tour patrons will feel as if they bumped into someone, only to find that there wasn't anyone standing next to them. Other occurrences in the tunnel are cold breezes, unexplainable noises and shadows moving around with no source.

MINERAL SPRINGS HOTEL

This is one of my favorite spots in Alton. Not only for the great stories that are here, but also the nostalgia of this once-grand hotel. The hotel was opened in 1914. The building wasn't actually intended to be a hotel. Two brothers named Herman and August Luer owned a very profitable meat packaging plant. With the amount of meat they were packaging they found themselves in need of an ice plant where they could store the meat. In 1909, the brothers began excavation for the ice plant. That's when the construction crew struck a natural spring.

A chemist (no records were ever found on this guy) tested the water and said that it was definitely very high in minerals. He even went as far to suggest that the Luer brothers use this mineral water for a totally different business venture. Within four years, a hotel was built on the property instead of the previously planned ice plant. The venture was dubbed the Mineral Springs Hotel and people would come from all over the country to partake in its medicinal water.

During the early 1900s, people really bit into the idea of mineral water. Not only could you bathe in the healing waters, but you could also swim in it and drink it. This seemed very strange as the water had a very bad smell to it rivaling that of rotten eggs. But people didn't care and they flocked here making the Luers a lot of money in the process. Advertisements would speak of this "miracle" water curing everything that ails you. People would walk into the building all crippled and gangly (like Len) and would leave jumping for joy as they clicked their heels in glee.

The swimming pool was one of the largest in the country. Balls and parties would be frequently held at poolside. It was very common to see tuxedo- and evening gown-clad people mingling around the pool as an orchestra played in the background. This was in the regular pool. There was another swimming pool below that one. This pool was used by men only, primarily because they tended to swim nude.

Eventually the brothers began bottling the water and selling it all around the area. As if swimming in this awful smelling water wasn't enough, it's hard to believe that people actually drank the stuff. You'd have to think that by containing it a bottle, the smell would about knock you out as soon as you opened it. Regardless of the smell, the brothers did quite well with the water selling it as far south as New Orleans.

In the mid 1920s, the hotel was sold, but it continued to boast of its mineral water. It was actually quite the little surprise to see it hang on as long as it did. During World War II, attendance at the hotel diminished severely. Either people didn't go there because they were overseas fighting, or perhaps they were helping the war effort from home. It may have also been that people just weren't interested in a spa treatment because it was a somber time or perhaps gasoline rationing had something to do with it. Whatever it was, the times were tough for the hotel and the pool was closed around that time. The 1950s weren't any better as the hotel's condition began to decline. It was only going to be a matter of time before the hotel would shut down. That day came in 1971, when the hotel closed its doors for the first time in 57 years. It did, however, reopen in the late '70s when it became a mall housing several shops and cafes.

I have had the opportunity to visit this building several times after hours as well as on scheduled tours. There are a few main areas of interest that I'd like to discuss. Unfortunately, tales sometimes change with the times. Usually it's because of these changes that a story either becomes more intriguing or it loses every ounce of truth it may have had. That is the case with this building. There are a lot of local legends that have been made up to add a human element to the hauntings that occur in the Mineral Springs Hotel.

It's difficult to capture the entire building in one shot (Photo by Bill Alsing)

One of the first areas of activity is the swimming pool. There are several different versions of this story that I have heard throughout the years. As far as which story is true, I really don't know for sure. I'll just lay them out there and let you judge for yourself.

The first version states that a husband and wife were staying at the hotel and were going to attend a lavish party around the pool. The husband went down first because the wife was taking too long to get ready. Upon arriving at the pool, she caught her husband being friendly with another female guest. The wife had been monitoring her husband's flirtatious ways for weeks and this seemed to be her breaking point. She walked over to the pair, removed her high-heeled shoe and hit her husband in the face with it. He grabbed at his face, stumbled into the pool and drowned.

The second version that I heard also speaks of a husband and wife at a pool party. Only in this one, the roles were reversed. The husband caught the wife in the arms of another man. When he confronted them, it turned into a wrestling match and the husband was thrown into the pool, where he drowned.

No matter which version you believe, they both have the same ending. Regardless, a male spirit has been seen around the pool for years. He is said to be very dressed up and usually has a very angry posture. Legend says that if you stand near the pool and he manifests himself, he will try to push you into the pool as an act of revenge. Trust me, as much as I'd like to see this ghost, being pushed into a pool that hasn't had any water in it for years, doesn't seem worth it to me. Some people also report that sometimes outside of the room where he was staying that fatal night, one can see a puddle of water take form. This puddle is said to be from his spirit returning to his room soaking wet. What a great addition to the story, but I don't think it's true. I could be wrong, but it seems like an attempt to add a more detail to the original haunting. A few years ago, I went on one of Troy's tours and we actually went down into the haunted pool. Troy did a great job setting the mood as he walked down into the pool with the soft glow of a lantern as the only light. It was on this tour that "Crazy" Steve saw a person leaning against a pillar. Within seconds the form just kind of faded away into the darkness. As we were all leaving the pool area that night, Steve inspected each of our clothes to see if it had been one of us standing by the pillar. It wasn't.

    Another time I was on a tour of the pool, we were all standing around listening to stories. All of a sudden, the door to the pool area opened and closed. This door is very heavy and when it shuts, it slams! This really scared everybody on the tour. As if the door wasn't enough, we also heard footsteps walking around the pool. Several people shined their lights on the wall but there was nobody there. We were all accounted for in the pool area and the door was too heavy for a gust of air to blow it open. We had no idea how to debunk this activity so I think that we were part of something very special. It was very tense for those of us who were there. There were about forty people all trapped in this area with a single staircase as our only route of escape. As I always state on my tours, I am not above knocking someone down to save myself. I'll usually go for an injured person or some other weak target. When I get scared, it's all about survival of the fittest!

    A second spirit that haunts the hotel involves the mural painted around one of the hallways of the building. Legend says that there was a guest who was down on his luck and was unable able to pay his bill. The tenant worked out a deal to paint the mural as a form of payment. Unfortunately he died before the mural was finished. Even though the mural was unfinished, the man's spirit never quit. Eventually, through several appearances of the ghost artist, the mural was finished.

This story is actually not true. The man who painted the mural did do it to pay his bill, but he finished the job and moved on in our world and not the spirit world. There is, however, a spirit that frequents the former bar area. I think this legend was designed to help explain who the spirit is that has been seen. Sometimes by adding a human element to a story, it makes it easier to cope with the idea of ghosts. That seems to be the case here. The spirit is described as an average-sized male, sometimes looking confused, (some would say drunk) but never displaying a threatening demeanor.

This third spirit involves a tragic love triangle. There are a couple of versions of this story. Each version has the same beginning and ending, but the middle section differs. The tale begins with a husband and wife who were staying in the hotel. The husband was in Alton on business because he was a traveling salesman. His wife was there to keep him company. With the amount of time that the husband was out selling, the wife became a little, well, bored. It was because of this boredom that she found somebody to help occupy her time (you do the math on this one.)

One day, the husband came home a bit earlier than usual and he found his wife in the arms of another man. A grand argument broke out between the two as the other man somehow slipped out of the hotel undetected. The argument spilled out into the hallway and ended at the top of the stairs. The story differs at this point as some people say that the husband pushed the wife down the stairs and others say she tripped down the stairs. Either way, she ended up landing on her neck halfway down the stairs. The fall ended with her lifeless body sprawled across the base of the stairs. Her neck broke the second it hit the marble staircase.

Another story was created that branched off from the end of the previous tale. Some people say that after the woman hit the bottom of the steps, the husband was so distraught that he went into his room and committed suicide. This story isn't true and was only added to extend this already tragic tale. The true version of this story is that the husband stepped over his wife's body, went to the front desk and said his wife tripped and fell downstairs. The police arrived, ruled it an accident and the husband went on with his business.

This female spirit has been named the "Jasmine Lady." Her name was generated from the perfume she wore while she was alive. It's this same scent that lets you know she's around even in death. The most common ghostly activity is the scent of jasmine around the marble staircase. Some people have even reported seeing a woman falling down the stairs only to see her disappear once she reaches the bottom. I have actually smelled the fragrance on two occasions, once during a tour and once while shopping at the mall. You don't have to have high tech equipment to experience a ghost. Even when you are just out and about, you still have four very important tools for ghost hunting - your eyes, ears, nose, and touch.

One other story that I like to tell about the hotel involves former tenants who used to operate a store in the lower area of the mall. They told us about all the activity they had been experiencing during their stay in the building. While the shop was open during the day, items would fly off the shelves, the radio would turn itself on, disembodied voices would be heard and the front door would open on its own. One night after the store had closed for the evening, the owner was cleaning up. She went into the bathroom to wash her hands and upon trying to leave, the door wouldn't open. The door locks from the inside. The lady kept trying to open the door but it wouldn't budge. Just then she heard the giggle of a little girl on the other side of the door. The woman started to think that maybe a little girl had been left in the store or maybe she wandered in after it was closed. Whichever reason it was that brought the girl into the store didn't matter as the woman just wanted to get out of the bathroom. Every time she asked the girl to open the door, giggles would be the only response she'd get. Finally, after a few minutes of struggling with the door to the tune of the child's laughter, it clicked open. When the woman stepped out of the bathroom she saw the feet of the girl turn down an aisle. She began to follow the child all over the store. The whole time she'd only see the legs and feet, or she would hear giggles. Eventually the child led her to the back of the store where the noise and visions stopped. The woman stood there for a bit, listening and watching. Without warning, the laughter began right behind her. Without turning to look, the woman threw her hands up and ran straight out the door. I think a child's laughter can be the sweetest thing, but in the wrong situation and at the wrong time, it can be downright eerie.

THE CRACKER FACTORY

In 1866, H.N. Kendall built a large cracker factory in the city of Alton. When settlers came through Alton on their way west, they knew things weren't going to come easy. If game was scarce or fishing was tough, chances were they weren't going to survive the wild. Or, in the same respect, if the settlers weren't good at gathering food, it was going to be a tough go. Once you got past St. Louis you were on your own. There weren't any convenience stores, you couldn't run to a grocery store when you needed food, you were in the Wild West. That's a big reason why crackers played such an important role in the survival of the early settlers. Crackers would last indefinitely. I can't say that these crackers saved many lives, but I bet they helped get people by when times were tough.

During the factory's heyday, they were producing about 150 barrels of crackers a day. Five large brick ovens in the basement of the building were used for baking crackers. On the first floor was a small shop where Kendall sold his wares. All was going well and Kendall was making a lot of money with his factory until the early 1900s when the building was sold. Crackers were no longer needed by settlers because civilization had taken hold farther out west and railroads and refrigerated cars were commonplace.

The building was bought by Henry McPike who rented out the different rooms to various businesses. From that point on, there have been doctors' offices, insurance offices, general stores and antique shops located in the building. Since the 1970s it has been mostly antique stores. Most of the ghost stories have come about during the antique store days.

In the 1970s, Sam Thames took over the basement of the building where he opened up an antique store. Thames immediately started experiencing ghostly activity. He heard footsteps that would go up and down the staircase when there wasn't anyone in the store. Unfortunately, Sam passed away in the early 1990s and, some will tell you, he became one of the spirits that haunt the building.

In 2002 the building was rented out yet again by an aspiring antique seller. Riverbend Antiques officially opened its doors in November of that year. The space was small, but the proprietors made creative use of it. Three of the original cracker ovens were still in place and these were used for displaying antiques. Even while setting up prior to opening, they realized there was something special about the place. Other tenants began telling them about some of the strange happenings in the building. At first they just shrugged it off but it didn't take long for the ghosts to make themselves known.

I had the opportunity to investigate the store with the group I used to be involved with around 2002-2003. The owner told us about how she frequently heard footsteps in the building. Usually she would hear the front door to the store open and then she'd hear footsteps coming down the staircase, but there would never be anyone there. She also told me about all the times she replaced the thermostat because she thought it was defective. When she'd come into work the thermostat would be turned all the way up or all

A recent look at the Cracker Factory Building (Photo by Bill Alsing)

the way down. This would happen when she knew it hadn't been left that way the night before. Other occurrences were radios changing stations overnight, the open sign found turned around in the morning and items disappearing. One other common occurrence was the sound of someone whistling. It wasn't like someone was whistling a tune; it was more like someone just whistling to make noise. According to the owner, she could handle everything else, but the whistling was very annoying.

Not only was our team investigating that night, but WLCA radio at Lewis and Clark College in Godfrey, Ill., was making a live broadcast of the event. There were only a few things that happened that night. One probably wasn't anything paranormal, but was just my imagination getting the best of me. There was an old painting of a child and for some reason this thing just really creeped me out. I am not sure why it was, but I felt like he was just looking at me wrong. If it wasn't the painting giving me the weird vibes it may have been the old clown costume or old wedding dress that were hanging across from the painting that night. Whatever it was gave me goose bumps.

Some of our team members were able to capture some possible orbs on camera, but that wasn't the best thing that happened that night. Two of the disc jockeys went upstairs to record a segment in one of the rooms. They were up there by themselves for a bit while the rest of us were down in the basement. All of a sudden I heard loud banging noises and I heard a door crash open upstairs. I ran up the basement stairs which lead directly out to Broadway. Upon reaching the sidewalk I looked to my right and saw the two DJs running full speed down the street. I started down the street after them. Like Hansel and Gretel leaving breadcrumbs in the woods, the two scaredy cats were leaving bits and pieces of their MP3 recording device on the sidewalk for me to follow. I finally caught up with them in front of the Mineral Springs Hotel. I found this funny as they ran from one haunted location to an even more haunted location.

When I asked them what happened they said they were recording in one of the second floor apartments. While they were in there they kept hearing something moving around in the room next to them. They started to make their way to the room when all of a sudden they heard a growling noise and they took off running. They burst out of the room, flew down the stairs and kicked the door to the street open. Then along the way, they dropped the MP3 recorder.

I had them show me which room they were in when they heard the noise. They were glued to my side like my daughter is when she is around strangers. Once we got in the room I had them calm down and be quiet for a moment while I listened. Sure enough I heard some noises coming from the neighboring room. I walked into the room where the noises came and found the cause. They were doing some remodeling on the second floor. All the windows were open and the floor was covered with a protective plastic tarp. When the wind blew through the room, it caused the tarp to move about and it did sound like a growl. Unfortunately these two guys were scared by a five-pound tarp. Not only that, but the MP3 recorder was an innocent victim of the tarp's antics. The rest of the night was relatively quiet for us.

Riverbend Antiques has closed its doors after only a few years in business. We are hoping someone else rents the space soon so that we may possibly be able to bring our tours inside the building for a look. I am sure when the time comes for a new owner, Troy, Len and I will be knocking on the door asking if we can come in. As long as the door doesn't get slammed in our face in the first couple of minutes, we should be okay.

PIECE OF CAKE THEME PARTIES

This was one of my favorite stops on the tours and it had nothing to do with the fact that they gave us brownies as we were leaving. Okay, that did have a lot to do with me enjoying the place. In fact, my wife was more accepting of me coming home late from the tour when I emptied out my backpack revealing several brownies as they tumbled onto the table. Aside from the fact that the owners provided us a place to come inside, sit down, drink some coffee and hot cocoa and even indulge in the aforementioned brownies, this place is also extremely haunted.

To explain this business location would require me telling you what was formerly there. You see, this was previously known as the Meridian Coffee House, one of THE most haunted spots in

Alton. Very seldom did we go there with a tour and not have something happen. A lot of times, the spirits would let us know they were there in a very dramatic fashion. I'll get into that a bit later as now is the time for some history.

The Meridian as of today (Photo by Bill Alsing)

We have no idea why this location is haunted. As far as we know, there hasn't been any kind of traumatic event that took place here. Not to say that it takes a traumatic event to cause a haunting, but that is a major source. The only thing that we could find that would remotely tie to anything painful would be the stories of a field hospital that once stood on the grounds. This field hospital came before the building that we know of was even constructed. The hospital was set up to help treat Alton citizens who fell victim to the influenza epidemic that raged through the country in 1918. I suppose there were some deaths in the hospital, but that is only an assumption on my part as I do not know for sure.

The current building was constructed in the 1920s. Throughout the years, the building was used as offices, cafés and apartments. The ghost stories started in the late 1990s when the building was purchased by a man and woman who had the desire to open up a coffee shop. They wanted it to be a cool place for teens to come and hang out after school. It was intended to get kids off the street by giving them a fun place to be with their friends. Whether they were studying or listening to some of the live entertainment, this was a great place to be. And the ghosts seemed to like it, too!

While the building was being set up as a coffee shop, several things happened. Most common were the sounds of footsteps on the second floor when no one was up there. Items would disappear, only to reappear days later in areas where they wouldn't have been left. Any time spent alone in the building would leave you with the feeling of not being alone. These were the less dramatic occurrences.

One of my favorite stories about this building happened in 1998. In order to give it a European café feel, tables would often be put out on the sidewalk for patrons to sit and drink their coffee. After closing for the night, the staff began bringing in the tables from outside. The owner was sitting in the office counting the money from the register. She saw movement out of the corner of her eye and immediately looked at the security camera. She saw two employees carrying in the tables as they had been told. Oddly, she saw a third individual walk directly behind the workers and straight up the stairs. It appeared that the workers had no idea that someone had walked past them. Quickly, the owner came out of the office to see who it was. She went up the stairs as one of the employees ran up the outside fire escape. These were the only two ways out of the second floor. When they reached the upstairs they found no one. The person on the camera was described as a tall man with dark hair, wearing a striped or plaid shirt and jeans. This wouldn't be the last time he would make himself known.

The spirit was also seen sitting in one of the side rooms on the second floor. He was rocking back and forth in a chair just minding his own business. Once he was spotted, he slowly disappeared. There have also been unexplained shadows seen moving across the walls.

After several years, the Meridian closed its doors. We were very upset by this as it was a great place to go to and it was very rich with ghost stories. Thankfully it wasn't closed for long. This time it was to be known as Piece of Cake Theme Parties.

The owners Nikki and Laurie accepted us with open arms! Their business was thriving due to the paranormal angle. They would host overnight parties quite often. These parties would involve experimenting with Ouija boards, tarot cards and séances. Nikki and Laurie were great and we appreciated everything they did for us.

So many things were happening when we brought the tours

there. Len and I had a routine that we used to do when we got the groups into the building. As everyone was getting situated with drinks and brownies, Len and I would run up to the second floor and take a look around. We started doing this because several times, when we would leave the second floor and then come back to it, the furniture would change position. Usually when this happened, it was a piece of furniture moving just a couple of feet. On one occasion however, a chair moved clear across the room. Some people may think that it was someone on the tour doing it, but I can guarantee you it wasn't. When we have a group leave the second floor to go downstairs, we always do a walkthrough and take note of the surroundings. Because of this practice, we would have noticed the difference.

Once we got everyone seated, we would begin to tell the history of the building. We'd then divide into two groups and head upstairs. While we were telling the ghost stories to one group, the other would be partaking of the delicious brownies I spoke of earlier. Did I mention they made cheesecake brownies too? Once the ghost stories were done and people had an opportunity to walk around, we would switch the groups and do the stories over again. Sometimes the second group would have experiences because the energy was still left over from the first group. This atmosphere actually felt electric!

There was one occasion where I was giving a tour to a great group of people. As I was standing on the second floor telling some stories, the bathroom door in the little hallway behind where I was slammed shut. It even made me jump. I walked down the hallway with a couple of people and we looked at the door. This door was on a very heavy spring. There was no way that a breeze could have blown it open and cause it to slam. We then walked farther into the bathroom and it was definitely empty. This activity happened a lot to Len and me on the tours. Perhaps the spirit thought we were full of BS and that's why he slammed the bathroom door. I think a flush of the toilet may have gotten the same point across.

Quite a few times inside this building I would see things happen around people as they listened to the stories. It was really difficult not to point it out to them. I try not to do that because if I make a big deal out of something ghostly, then that's going to really frighten everyone. That's when someone will take off running and get hurt. If we ever see something, we just try to keep moving on with the story and pretend it didn't happen. Trust me, when something does happen, we'll tell you later.

On another occasion, as we directed the second group back down the stairs, Len and I began to sweep the area of leftover tourists. Once we confirmed that the area was clear, Len and I began making our way to the stairs. All of a sudden I heard the sound of hard soled shoes walking across a wooden floor right behind us. First off, the floor is carpeted so there's no way it cold have been us. I looked at Len and he was smiling. I asked if heard that and he nodded his head yes. We walked back to the center of the room and it was like we walked into a meat locker. We were freezing and both of were getting the goose bumps. Usually things don't happen to me. That's what made this experience so great! Not only did I have something unexplained happen, but Len had the same thing happen to him as well! I think we were both part of something very special that evening.

My favorite story to tell about the Meridian involved a little ten-year-old boy. This kid was great the whole evening. He had the big deer eyes and you could tell that he was soaking up every word. Len was giving the tour that night and I was on hand as the caboose. When we got everyone into the building, I immediately went upstairs to take a look at the furniture positioning. I was up there for a couple of minutes when I got a tingling sensation. I realized at this point I needed to use the bathroom. I went downstairs only to find that someone was already in there. I, being patient, waited my turn. As the door opened, that little boy cut me off and rushed into the restroom. That really wasn't that big of a deal to me, but the fact that he didn't shut the door was a little rude. Here Len was trying to tell a story, and we were being serenaded by the sound of this boy using the toilet. There was a girl near the bathroom door so I motioned to her to pull it shut. As she did so, the sound from inside instantly ceased. The door flew open and this pale-faced, scared-to-death boy came running out straight to his mother's side. I chuckled a bit as I made my way into the restroom.

Unfortunately Piece of Cake Theme Parties closed its doors a couple of years ago and the building has been empty ever since. This year it appears that they are completely gutting it. I'm not sure what new business will be coming there, but hopefully it will allow us to enter through the doors once again. This location truly never let us down.

FIRST UNITARIAN CHURCH

The First Unitarian Church was built in the early 1830s. It was then called St. Matthew's and was of the Catholic denomination when it first opened its doors. Unfortunately, a fire broke in 1855 and destroyed the building. A new Catholic church was built across town. The only part of the original church that remained was the foundation. The new Catholic church was called Saints Peter and Paul and was located on a piece of land the townspeople dubbed "Christian Hill." The previous church property was sold to the Unitarians and was renamed The First Unitarian Church. To show people's feelings toward the Unitarian faith, the site of the Unitarian Church was popularly called "Heathen Hill."

The Unitarians worshipped for many years at that location. That is, until tragedy struck when the church had nearly reached its 50-year anniversary. In 1904, another fire broke out, and once again the building was destroyed, leaving only the foundation. It was rebuilt shortly afterwards and finally, on the third attempt, the church remains to this day. Every time I think about this story, it reminds me of "Monty Python and the Holy Grail." Each time the landowner built his castle on the swamp, it sank. That is, until he built the third one, which was the strongest castle in the world.

Now common knowledge in Alton is that a previous minister, Phillip Mercer of the First Unitarian Church, committed suicide inside the church in 1934. His body was found hanging from the transom above the entrance to his study by a member of the congregation. There was no suicide note and no known motive for him to have been murdered. Mercer was loved by all those he came in contact with. He was a gentle, loving man and he was well respected by his peers. With such a tragic event as a man taking his own life, there certainly is the groundwork here for a genuine haunting.

Reports of music playing in the sanctuary run rampant.

The church exterior resembles that of a castle (Photo by Bill Alsing)

Visitors to the church have heard the sound of footsteps walking around when no one else was there. Sometimes the scent of men's cologne fills the air as a cold draft blows past. There have been reports of shadows lurking around the Wuerker Room. Not just any shadows, these are shadows of a tall, slender person, similar in build to the late Reverend Mercer. Former ministers have even reported noticing a man standing near a pew in the back of the church, only to see him disappear as they approached. All of these anecdotes make for great stories to tell, especially since we have experienced these things first-hand during our tours.

We also know that the basement is a very haunted area. In the early years of the church's existence, school was held there. We also believe, as you have already read, that the basement may have been a stop on the Underground Railroad. One aspect I'd like you to consider is this theory: when the fire ravished this church in the 1850s, who's to say that there weren't some slaves hiding in the secret room? Perhaps they lost their lives during the blaze. We don't know this for sure, but I can tell you that we have heard screams coming from the basement on a few occasions.

If you are interested in going into the depths of the church, by all means take our Extended Ghost Hunters' Tour of Alton. The church basement is one of our extra perks on that tour.

I always make it my business to bring a lantern into the church when I conduct my tours. As people begin to file in, I head straight to the altar and place the lantern on the floor. It casts a soft glow over the sanctuary and really seems to help set the mood. I really enjoy speaking at the church primarily because it's quiet, I don't have to yell and I can just tell the story in a dramatic, uninterrupted fashion.

Frequently, we have a lot of activity occur while I am speaking to the crowd. Most often the activity is either in the back of the church or behind me in the Wuerker Room. The activity in the back of the church involves a lot of shadows moving across the wall. On several occasions as I am speaking, I'll just see the shadow of a person move across the wall. The only light is coming from the lantern to my left. In order to make that shadow, someone would have to be walking in the last few rows of pews. Obviously, I can tell if someone is walking around and I know that wasn't the case when I saw the shadows.

I've also seen the doors to the church opening by themselves. This hasn't happened too often, but when it does happen, it always catches me off guard. Sometimes I'll see a tour participant turn around, catch the doors' movement, and then turn back towards me with wide eyes. I just keep going like I didn't see a thing.

After I tell the history of why we think the church is haunted, I begin to tell the ghost stories. During October 2006, I had a young lady named Courtney Colvin come on the tour with her parents. They were sitting in the very front pew to my right. I must say that I have never had someone sit in that area before. Directly behind me to my right is a set of folding doors that lead to the Wuerker Room. Throughout my stories, Courtney was taking pictures. As I got further into the ghostly happenings, I mentioned how a lot of times when we speak, people will see

There is a shadow in the shape of a person on the back right (Photo by Steve Mangin)

Here is a zoomed in look at the shadow (Photo by Steve Mangin)

The Lighter Side of Darkness -- Page 132

dark shadows move around the room behind me.

Courtney's reaction at this point was priceless. She began hitting her mom on the leg as she became very excited. I stopped telling the story because I was laughing and I asked her what was wrong. She got up and showed me two photos on her digital camera that she had just taken. The first photo was completely normal. You can see how the flash lit up the doorframe and wall. The light also went through the doorway and illuminated the back room floor, wall and ceiling. In the second picture, you see a black mass that takes up about seventy five percent of the doorway. It also appears as though the mass is creeping out and onto the doorframe. The flash still lights up the back room ceiling and wall as well as the doorframe, so it's not a flash issue. I really can't explain it, but it is by far one of the most intriguing photos someone has taken on one of my tours.

That wasn't the only neat thing that happened to us that night. After we finished in the sanctuary, we all got up and moved into that back room. We like to go back there to tell more stories as well as point out where Reverend Mercer hanged himself. On this night a girl unknowingly walked right under the spot where Mercer hanged himself. As soon as she did, she grabbed at her neck and stumbled away from the spot. It kind of looked as if she were trying to avoid a bee, wasp, locust, or some other kind of flying bug attack. When I asked her what happened, she said she felt something brush across her neck. It was a very interesting occurrence due to her location at the time she had the strange feeling. I also had a girl take a picture in that area and she captured an orb in motion. You could see there was movement on the digital image because it showed several balls of light that were all attached by a motion stream. It was a great photo as well.

We have had a lot of things happen on the extended tour when we go down into the basement. There was one night where I was the caboose so I had to follow the group down. Two guys were wandering around a bit taking photos so I had to round them up and usher them downstairs. We were far behind the rest of the tour by this point. When we walked down the short hallway to the top of the stairs, a door handle began to shake wildly. This door is always locked at night so I knew there was no

Here is the first shot of the door (Photo by Courtney Colvin)

Notice the dark mass that blocks the lower part of the doorway (Photo by Courtney Colvin)

way anyone could have gotten into the room. I checked the door to make sure it was locked and of course it was. I shined my light inside the door window and the room was completely empty. Whatever it was definitely got the attention of all three of us. When the activity happened, all three of us instinctively backed up against the wall!

Once we were lined up on the wall, I began to size up the other guys to see which one I could effectively knock down and feed to the ghoulies. Fortunately, we all made it through the experience fine.

On another occasion I was in the basement with a group of about twenty people. I began telling them about the TLC experience in the center of the basement. Everyone formed a circle around me as I began my tale. When I tell this story, I always like to turn out all the lights so people can see how dark it is down there.

On this particular night, I was being overly dramatic with the story so it became very tense. Just then this girl to my left let out an ear-piercing scream. That whole side of the circle caved in and began bumping into me and the rest of the group. I quickly turned on my lantern and started looking behind her to see what scared her. I always found this funny that I didn't bother seeing if the scared girl was okay, I was too busy trying to see what weird creature did the scaring. Well it turned out that the girl's cell phone began to vibrate and she thought it was something pulling on her clothes. It took me a good fifteen minutes to calm everyone down. People were laughing, crying, and drying out their pants after that one. She definitely scared the tour guide, which is what a lot of people like to try to do on our tours.

Since we are professionals (sometimes) we try to not scare people on purpose. But, there was this one time... In 2006, the Fall Festival was held in Alton at the bookstore. After the festival we did a dinner tour and then we all went to the church for an investigation. I was hanging out with a group in one of the basement classrooms. They were attempting to get EVPs, but it was very difficult because of all the foot traffic walking down the hallway into the older part of the basement. I could see their frustration building so I took it upon myself to try to alleviate the problem by scaring the living daylights out of them.

The door to the classroom has a window in the center of it. I peered out the window and saw a woman leaning against the far wall directly across from my window. Although I didn't think she was the one making the noise, she was going to be a victim of circumstance and also an example. I waited a couple of minutes for her to look toward the door but she never did. Finally, I decided to make her look. I began jiggling the doorknob just enough for her to look. As soon as her eyes met the door, I put my face in the window while holding a flashlight under my chin. Her jaw about hit the floor and I could tell she wanted to scream but was too overcome with fright to make a sound. I was just going to leave it at that, but I couldn't stop laughing and I did actually feel kind of bad. I had to go into the hall and apologize to her. She was a good sport and really did find it funny. Like I said, though, we don't normally do stuff like that. It was just too good of an opportunity to pass up.

As much as I love having the First Unitarian Church as the

last stop on the tour, it's tough on us during the Halloween season. By the time we get to the church we have been walking for well over two hours. To get to the church, we have to walk up a massive two-block hill. Then, as if that's not bad enough, once you get to the top of the hill, you walk up some steps to actually get to the church entrance. By early November, Len and I are exhausted from walking that hill so many times. But I will say this: the church is the grand finale for us. Having the church as our last stop, when it's dark out and late at night, is a great way to end the evening. If you've ever been there, I'm sure you agree.

RETURN OF THE HISTORY AND HAUNTINGS BOOK COMPANY

At this point, we make our way back to the bookstore. A lot of people will go home, and some will shop and listen to more stories. Len and I love telling stories. There have been times where we've stayed an extra couple of hours because people want more stories. We call this part of the tour "The Bonus Coverage" segment. I really enjoy people and it means the world to me to see people really taking interest in our stories. So please, even if you have already been on the tour, come back and bring your friends. Let us know if you have been on the tour before and we can make up new stuff so it'll be a different experience for you! Okay, just kidding about that part, but we are always adding new stories to our tours. So I'm sure it'll be different every time you come.

Lessons Learned

1. Enjoy what you do and others will enjoy you doing it.

2. Troy who? You say he lived in Alton? Never heard of him.

WHY DO I DO THIS?

This is one of the most frequently asked questions I get. I think we do this because we want to find answers. I don't care what anyone says, I don't think there are experts in this field. There are people, however, that have been doing this longer than others. If there were experts, I'd think we'd have the answers by now.

In a way, I kind of hope we don't find the answers. I'm having way too much fun trying to find the answers and I don't want that fun to stop. It's kind of like when I play golf. I love playing, but I don't want to get better than I am now. If I get better and have an off day, I'll want to give the game up. In the case of paranormal investigations, I think when the answers are found, we may not be needed any longer. That seems like a strange theory, but I'll stand by it. Imagine looking for the answers and yet hoping you don't find them. Now that's paranormal.

I hope you enjoyed this book. I'm glad I was able to share some of my experiences with people who don't get to hear them from me in person. To those of you I haven't met, what are you waiting for? Get out to Alton and go on one of the best ghost tours in the country. I'm not just saying that either. I really do mean it. It'll be the best three hours of your life. Believe It!

Until next time, be well and Happy Hauntings!

Luke Naliborski
Summer 2007

ABOUT THE AUTHOR
LUKE NALIBORSKI

Luke Naliborski is a paranormal investigator from the St. Louis, MO and Illinois area. He is also the Investigations Coordinator for the American Ghost Society, a member of Prime Investigations (Paranormal Researches In the Metro East) and a guide for the Alton Hauntings Ghost Tours. Luke's experiences has taken him to numerous haunted locations throughout the past 10 years --- some good, some bad, but most end up being quite entertaining.

Luke was born and raised in Belleville, Illinois. Later he moved to Marissa, IL and currently lives in Mascoutah, IL with his gorgeous, understanding wife Heather and their beautiful daughter Iris. In his spare time, Luke plays piano, he's an eraser-carrying golfer, and he also plays hockey. The rest of his time, also thought of as quality time, is spent with his family.

Growing up his childhood interests in ghost stories guided him to the place in life where he is right now. Instead of just reading the stories, he now has his own. It's his desire in life to share these stories in any form he can. Although Luke usually tells his stories through lecturing or nights around the campfire, this is his first attempt at a book. Hopefully, there'll be more to follow.

ABOUT WHITECHAPEL PRESS

Whitechapel Productions Press is a division of Dark Haven Entertainment and a small press publisher, specializing in books about ghosts and hauntings. Since 1993, the company has been one of America's leading publishers of supernatural books and has produced such best-selling titles as Haunted Illinois, The Ghost Hunters Guidebook, Ghosts on Film, Confessions of a Ghost Hunter, Resurrection Mary, Bloody Chicago, The Haunting of America, Spirits of the Civil War and many others.

With nearly a dozen different authors producing high quality books on all aspects of ghosts, hauntings and the paranormal, Whitechapel Press has made its mark with America's ghost enthusiasts.

Whitechapel Press is also the publisher of the acclaimed Ghosts of the Prairie magazine, which started in 1997 as one of the only ghost-related magazines on the market. It continues today as a travel guide to the weird, haunted and unusual in Illinois. Each issue also includes a print version of the Whitechapel Press ghost book catalog.

You can visit Whitechapel Productions Press online and browse through our selection of ghostly titles, plus get information on ghosts and hauntings, haunted history, spirit photographs, information on ghost hunting and much more. by visiting the internet website at:

www.prairieghosts.com

Or call us toll-free at 1-888-446-7859 to order any of our titles.
Discounts are available to retail outlets and online booksellers!

ILLINOIS AND AMERICAN HAUNTINGS TOURS

Whitechapel Press (and Dark Haven Entertainment) is the headquarters for the Illinois Hauntings Tour Co, offering the following ghost tours:

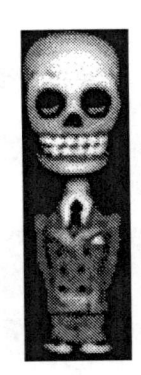

Alton Hauntings Ghost Tours / Alton, Illinois
Created by Troy Taylor, these tours are an interactive experience that allow readers to visit the historically haunted locations of the city and can be booked every year from April through October. Hosted by Len Adams, Luke Naliborski & Troy Taylor --- http://www.altonhauntings.com

Weird Chicago Tours / Chicago, Illinois
Created by Troy Taylor and based on his book Weird Illinois from Barnes & Noble Press, this is an alternative tour of Chicago, offering visitors the chance to see the other side of the city. Visit Chicagos most haunted sites, most notorious crime spots, most unusual places and much more! Available all year round!
http://www.weirdchicago.com

Haunted Decatur Ghost Tours / Decatur, Illinois
Created by Troy Taylor in 1994, these are the third longest running ghost tours in the state of Illinois! Visit the citys most haunted spots and take a nightime stroll through Greenwood Cemetery! Available April - October! http://www.haunteddecatur.com

American Hauntings Ghost Tours
Created by author Troy Taylor these tours offer Haunted Overnight Excursions to ghostly places around the Midwest and throughout the country. Available all year round!
http://www.illinoishauntings.com

Springfield Hauntings Ghost Tours / Springfield, Illinois
Join us in the Prairie States haunted Capital City for Springfields only authentic ghost tours. Experience the hauntings of Abraham Lincoln, the Springfield Theater Center and much more! Available April through October and hosted by John Winterbauer ----
http://www.springfieldhauntings.com